About the Author

Liesel was raised an only child in Lesotho with a small-town existence to follow. After her studies, her career took her to Cape Town where her son was born. A career as an executive assistant marked her as a career-orientated woman and the demands left her in tumultuous waters, leading to divorce. Life was then focused on her career which brought balance and stability. Only after her life-changing encounters with God in this period did a foundation in her Christian walk truly establish. She believes in continual growth and living a life of impact.

Lady in a Corner

LIESEL KORB

Lady in a Corner

Olympia Publishers
London

www.olympiapublishers.com
OLYMPIA PAPERBACK EDITION

Copyright © LIESEL KORB 2024

The right of LIESEL KORB to be identified as author of this work has been asserted in accordance with sections 77 and 78 of the Copyright, Designs and Patents Act 1988.

All Rights Reserved

No reproduction, copy or transmission of this publication may be made without written permission.
No paragraph of this publication may be reproduced, copied or transmitted save with the written permission of the publisher, or in accordance with the provisions of the Copyright Act 1956 (as amended).

Any person who commits any unauthorised act in relation to this publication may be liable to criminal prosecution and civil claims for damage.

A CIP catalogue record for this title is available from the British Library.

ISBN: 978-1-83543-031-6

The information in this book has been compiled by way of general guidance only. Neither the author nor the publisher shall be liable or responsible for any loss or damage allegedly arising from any information or suggestion in this book.

First Published in 2024

Olympia Publishers
Tallis House
2 Tallis Street
London
EC4Y 0AB

Printed in Great Britain

Dedication

Dedicated to God, my Abba Father, Who holds my existence in His Hand.

Acknowledgments

THANK YOUS AND GRATITUDE. A journey is many a time a walk of solitude and done in isolation. But in the grace of our absolutely good Abba Father, He always provides wise counsel and people to provide input along the way in your walk. Mine was no different. I am exceptionally grateful to all those who had an indelible contribution to where I am today and whose part in my journey remains irreplaceable.

Mom – For all your ceaseless prayers and invaluable support in every way possible.

Wynand and Alica (my children) – For all the "blood, sweat and tears," ears and encouragement and the physical support whenever I needed it.

Lilla van Graan – For your doors that were and still are always open whenever I call. Your selfless love and your unselfish sharing and caring in times that I needed it most.

Riette Barnard – For messages that arrived at times when I needed it most and opening your heart and home whilst I was finding my way through the myriad of plans.

Sharon Kunneman – For the invaluable input and support from you and Shaun, even with the editing of this book.

"Amari" – For the unmistakable contribution towards my journey of faith, the "sounding board" for my writings and being a prayer partner of note.

Copyright

All scripture quotations have been taken from the Christian Standard Bible®, Copyright © 2017 by Holman Bible Publishers, unless otherwise indicated. Used by permission. Christian Standard Bible® and CSB® are federally registered trademarks of Holman Bible Publishers.

Scripture taken from the New King James Version® is marked NKJV. Copyright © 1982 by Thomas Nelson. Used by permission. All rights reserved.

Chapter 1
Introduction

This book is for every individual who ever doubted that they would see a tomorrow or that tomorrow could bring change and life.

My story is written on instruction, with part of me in the present and part of me reflecting on the way. It is consciously done in two dimensions – past reflection and present instruction. Life doesn't come with clear instructions, albeit that guidance from the Father is available, humans tend to lean on their own understanding and desires. Especially, when their faith has no firm foundation. Wisdom is but wise in our own eyes.

This book is not for the faint hearted or the lukewarm believer. This is for the individual who wants to reach full maturity in the spirit, who wants a true and heartfelt relationship with Jesus Christ, the Holy Spirit and God, the Father. If you want to hear and understand the art to listen and hear, please keep reading.

The human soul knows the difference between right and wrong yet is overruled by the desires of the flesh and weak knowledge in understanding the spirit. If only we are taught how to silence these desires of the flesh at a young age and taught to learn and understand hearing the spirit. To truly yield and understand the pressing into spirit, the One true Creator of Heaven and Earth.

Instructions are only found when the student is ready. A little bit of irony, no? We need instructions to yield to spirit – yet, do we know that we should? And where to go to hear, to listen and how? This is an alien concept compared to the pleasures of this world. Of course, we have all heard that the evil one also uses spiritual means, dark forces, and influences to derail our lives. However, do we in the daily course of events stop and evaluate any incidents or people truly when a situation is presents that which we've always hoped or dreamt of? Mostly and sadly not, when facts on the table at that given time presented seemingly good ground.

This book aims at evaluating daily life, things that seem good and natural on the surface but below are fraught with disturbing agendas and the work of the enemy. How to discern, and recognize, signs of the evil one at work, vocabulary and words that kill and destroy.

But most importantly, how to find the answers in the Living Word when you are alone in a corner, and you have only yourself to depend on, to understand how to stand up again.

Chapter 2
Background

I was born and raised in Maseru, Lesotho, as an only child to Afrikaner parents. At the time, Lesotho was still very much a British colony with many missionaries. This was a wonderful background toward a cosmopolitical atmosphere filled with excitement and culture. Friends were grounded in faith and a solid base was formed during my early years in a British nursery school and the Methodist Church.

My upbringing was in English and only later was Afrikaans part of my vocal existence, hence, being in an English-medium school, but I matriculated with both languages as first language – which stood me in great stead with my career choices.

As an only child, it could be said that my standards of upbringing and the privilege of my environment was very different to those of my peers in terms of culture, views on life, exposure to belief systems and a worldly view over cross cultural spectrums.

It was, therefore, with great trepidation that the move across the border into South Africa's little town Ladybrand transpired. This small-town existence created its own set of rules as well as an immense clash with small mindedness on more than one occasion. My high school life was not pleasant and, on many occasions, I was the total outcast struggling to find my way.

My college years brought me back to city life in Bloemfontein, where my equilibrium was moderately established. After three years of studying as an executive assistant, I entered the work force and met my Afrikaner husband (with Dutch parents). This culminated in moving to Cape Town and my son was born.

The early years of married life was reasonable, yet it quickly became evident that the absolute clash of two cultures had its detrimental effect. My inherent English upbringing as well as the mostly English corporate world soon had me in an emotional turmoil of being two people with an everyday battle of the mind of who I really was. This identity crisis reared its ugly head. Several factors contributed to me leaving this marriage after seventeen years, determined to work at my career and live in the only identity I truly could relate to and understand.

Soon after this, my journey with God truly started as a faith-filled one, where I was baptized as an adult and baptized with the Holy Spirit.

A whole new journey of life started.

Was this an easy road? No, definitely not.

The first four years were immensely rocky, to say the least, and I struggled to find my way. The obstacles of fresh trauma after the divorce as well as losing my son, to insecurities within myself and very real financial issues, work establishment and finding a new home was incredibly real. But it was the start. There was only one way and that was forward. Did I make mistakes and wrong decisions? Yes, hundreds!

Only when I found stability in God, and a good established position within an organization, did my life reach a point of an almost "smooth road" existence on a higher level. My confidence grew, my finances came into alignment. I worked hard to gain financial independence. It happened and my home was my sanctuary which started to reflect who I was becoming.

Looking back, I now also understand that my faith was growing and reaching a new level. But every level has its own devil! And we all know that the evil one uses people to derail and deceive those that walk upright in God. My life was no exception – especially at this point, where I was becoming healthier and moving into that which I believed God had in store for me.

The yearning for a life partner is a human desire, and mine was no different. After almost four years of not seeing anyone or finding that partner that I prayed for, I was introduced to a person I believed was everything I wanted. The next phase of my detrimental journey started.

At this point, I knew nothing about narcissism or the likes thereof. I had no conceivable idea of the concept or what it entailed, and my life was pretty much occupied in a bubble of secure ignorant bliss.

This journey of almost eleven years of absolute disillusion, heartache, deception, and lies had commenced.

Chapter 3
The Beginning

It goes without saying that we do not go through life believing the worst in our fellow human beings, until such time as the contrary is reflected, especially in a new relationship. It is only later in life and due to experience that trepidation and certain signs that are evident arise, which is contrary to our own belief system and values, that we acknowledge with great discernment that which is not right at the outset.

The freshness of the attention and the overwhelming flood of affection is the food for the drought we've been through and the water we have so desperately longed for. We walk in this "love bombing" and desire for more and totally oblivious to ever consider anything sinister or look for any warning signs. So eager to please and reciprocate, at any cost! And I mean, *any* cost.

For suddenly, this fun-filled world has opened, and you share heartily of yourself, your life, your family, your experiences, and your being.

Late night conversations are endless, sleepovers happen, and you believe that you have never experienced love at this level. And trust me, you haven't!

You give so much of yourself, and bend over backwards to please him, to just get the recognition you so crave! The place you really want is to be by his side, but he gives this to everybody (especially his children) but not to you. You work hard, spend your resources and time to support him in his ventures and his life.

Subtly he tells you what he wants, his desires, what he likes to see you wear – from your shoes to your underwear. You start to compromise, and to please. The words start with, "if you love me" or "look at what I do for you."

Somewhere in you, the process of losing your identity has started, but very subtly. Conflicts and differences of opinions are mine fields that result in spells of the silent treatment. You start to feel like a hare in the spotlight; not sure which way to turn and wondering what you've done wrong. The manipulation tactics are evident, but you still don't recognize the mind-games.

Many a time you consider to just walking away from it all, as it's just so difficult to reconcile the differences. You recognize them, and there are so tremendously many, yet you foolishly believe that love can conquer all. And on many an occasion you are told so in as many words! You try harder and give more. Deeper into the pit of dark oblivion.

You are clearly made to understand you are different. Things don't work the way you do them or say them. What you do or say is not normal. And in hindsight, in their frame of existence that statement had absolute merit, as it would never be normal in their framework of a culturally different existence. But at that time, it was said offensively and in an accusatory manner. To clearly indicate that there was an outcast in their midst – but please note in the same breath the outcast is "loved," albeit their definition of love. Double irony in this statement alone.

With great flair social get togethers were organized, which would result in an evening of drinking, laughing, and joking and inter alia comments made at my expense. This resulted in serious arguments behind closed doors afterwards. And in no uncertain terms the differences were again highlighted. In addition to this, all the conflicts of previous differences of opinions, were once again brought to the fore and used against me as examples of how insecure I am and how wrong my behavior was. I was clearly made to understand that I am the problem, as I couldn't "let my hair down" and sacrifice my standards. Which I was furthermore made to understand were absolutely ridiculous.

Why did I not leave at this stage? Was I in love with the thought of being in love?

In hindsight – most definitely! For it is only later, which I will elaborate on in the chapters that follow, that I will explain this.

Against all odds, a marriage proposal was made on a weekend away. When I dared to ask for the thoughts around a wedding date, I was shunned – very clearly and very definitely. I was told in no uncertain terms that this would be discussed at a later date. After three attempts at discussing this matter in a six-month period, no conclusions were reached and the sword over my head was always consistent. The reason being my non-compliance or non-conformance to his will or standards. At this point in time, I left and ended it all.

A period evolved at which point he returned to ask for another chance at this relationship. I agreed with certain provisos and very definite outlines of how I saw this moving forward. Many promises were made, and agreements suddenly reached! In my mind this was a new beginning, a new way forward, with a much better mutual understanding. Six years since we met, I believed the time had come that it would be different and the plethora of mistakes of the past would not be repeated. Little did I know!

After a holiday and getting engaged the second time, plans were made that I move into his home (of more than thirty years, bought whilst married to his ex-wife). I gave up all that I had and severed ties with the single life and home that I lived in for almost ten years. I had no plans to return, neither did I leave any backdoors open for me to revisit that space in my life.

Life in my mind was good and moving forward. It was time to create the new and truly build on this relationship. I relocated with an engagement ring on my finger, and this time round a wedding date was set.

Disaster struck from the day I walked into, what I thought would be "home" for a period, based on the promises made.

To my dismay. I found pornography – sufficient to fill a black bag. This confirmed some requests and conversations of the past. The conflict that erupted was not a pretty sight, and my standards were once again brought into the equation. I clearly recall the conversation. My reply to all the accusations was that if my standards were not up to scratch, I suggested he take it up with God as I live according to His standards. No reply was forthcoming.

The carpet ripped out from under me, was but a menial statement compared to the weight of the reality I was faced with.

How do I go from here?

This was one heavy aspect I was not prepared to tolerate under any circumstances in any way or form. I was just short of crucified on this matter.

I was submerged with unresolved rejection of the first round of promised marriage that didn't happen, the deception of the above and a multitude of questions started to grow. The doubts and the distrust started on absolutely every level imaginable!

From the so-called password on his cellphone, to me being discussed with his children and ridiculed, to his whereabouts and so-called colleague "acquaintance."

In my mind, there was just no way forward and the cookie started to crumble badly and vigorously. Many arguments ensued.

It is important that you understand that life was not always a conflict and there were periods that were pleasant and even joyful, albeit short-lived and few-and-far in between. Conflicts would arise out of the most mundane issues, due to an absolute clash of personality – or so I thought at the time.

I started to become aware that I was beginning to live a life of double existence – that of a chameleon.

I was Liesel from the moment I walked out the door in the morning, the Liesel that could live and breathe a life of professionalism and do "my normal" during the day. But the moment there was a get together and the so-called home environment, this changed completely.

It was shortly after the passing of my father on 1 April 2019 and the return of a road trip holiday of that year that I made some very serious decisions. On 19 June 2019, I went to church in the morning and afterwards approached Pastor Henry Pike, to pray over my current circumstances. We had a lengthy conversation, and my mind was pretty much set on what I was not going to tolerate any longer. I left the church and went to the hospital bed of a friend during visiting hours. I knew I needed to start moving towards becoming me and find my way.

At that time, I was newly appointed in a position, and this took everything I had to stay upright besides having to add the burden of the home life as well.

It goes without saying that not one promise was heeded or kept. But everything that was promised, swept under the proverbial carpet as inconsequential and then done for or with his children. That made my position very clear. A position of convenience, a means to an end, one who paid half of the holidays and whose vehicle was used on most road trips without taking responsibility for any maintenance thereof. Spoken to in times of need and fulfilling a basic role of housekeeping when required. And even in this time ridiculed, spoken down to and instructed on how to act and do within the framework of his version of correct.

I was chased out of his home on many an occasion and clearly reminded of the fact that it was his home, and I am the one who needs to leave. It was after such an occurrence that this hospital visit happened.

During our discussion in hospital, I was told to write my thoughts and my wishes down, what it is that I wanted to see. My comments were that God knows my thoughts, upon which I was corrected and made to understand that I should write and write detail of that which I wanted to see – in this the plan would become clear. And to be specific and not just ask for a man, or a way – I am to describe and say exactly what I wish to happen.

We still shared the joke about this, as my good friend also asked for a man in her life, and her words were that she would even cook and clean house for him if she was taken care of. Then she said to me, look where that got her – she is staying with her brother! She never detailed the specifics!

I went to the place called "home" and poured myself out over pages and pages of thoughts, instructions, and desires. I opened my Bible.

I started doing business with God.

He did business with me.

My journey began.

Chapter 4
The Journey – Growth in Faith

"Draw near to God, and he will draw near to you. Cleanse your hands, sinners, and purify your hearts, you double-minded" – James 4:8

God is more concerned about your character, than your comfort. In my case my discomfort.

At this point, I inherently knew there was something bigger than myself, that I needed to do, to enable me to walk away from my situation. I also knew that there was so much wrong in my decisions, the physical place I found myself, and my reality. How did I get to this messy doldrum of hollowness?

The landscape of my existence at that point was one of a person entangled in a spider's web in a corner. Literally and figuratively nowhere to go and no resources to depend on, except the salary that was deposited in my bank account at the end of each month. This was a factor that was vocally used as a weapon of emotional destruction to indicate the contrary in his favor. And that he could work with money, and to take note that he had money!

I was in a place of often contemplating suicide and the most effective way to do so. My outbursts of just wanting to be heard and acknowledged were met with indignation of insecurity. And I was ridiculed and accused of being irrational and mad.

My resources and means to resources were used to enable and establish my son in a business, when he expressed his wish to return to Cape Town after serious disillusionment of a life with his father. This could not have come at a worse time. I set my life and my emotions aside and focused solely on the future and the establishment of a business for my son, to get him on his feet as soon as possible.

A young man fraught with PTSD and serious rejection, the lack of funds and zero support from a father who chose his second wife above the interests of his son and made no qualms about admitting such.

This became a bone of contention in my circumstances in the home which I will refer to as "the madhouse." Which at any given time was criticized and compared to the so-called alternate picture of his fabulous offspring.

I chose tunnel vision and directed all my energy towards my son, the re-establishment of him and my future daughter-in-law in Cape Town, the move, finding a home for them and getting them, both set up with vehicles, phones, furniture and what they needed to start building a life.

Yes, you read correctly, and a fair amount of my furniture was incorporated into this project. A period of great testing followed, as a mother and as a believer.

The road was fraught with potholes, uphills, detours, and craters!

My existence became a very solitary one and my time was spent, between work, supporting my son on the phone (and to a degree financially) and ploughing all I had in me, into deepening my path with God.

I intentionally, at this point made it my business to understand the Word, but more so to find a teacher who would help me to get to grips with my growth. I spent hours and hours navigating YouTube and the internet, searching scriptures, and searching ways.

I wanted to know how.

I wanted to know more.

I wanted to know what I needed to do to make that in the Word, practical in my life.

I wanted to know how to get from there to out of there!

I started asking God to show me the mechanics.

I knew that I had to grow to find truth.

My search led me to various teachers, which in my ignorance at the time I did not recognize as teachers, but mere pastors that preach online. And I started to drink from that well.

I stumbled across Katie Souza, and her story was so radical and grabbed me that I was instantly hooked on her ministry and her messages were practical. She taught on how to heal and guard your soul in practical everyday language that I could get my head around. I listened day and night, every morning, and every evening whilst I was driving to work and from work. I couldn't dare listen in the "madhouse" as I was ridiculed, and heads just shaken when a whim of sound could be heard. I resorted to wearing earphones.

Through messages, I started to understand obedience, I started to understand what is possible against all odds. I had a glimpse of how big the God is that I profess to serve. My search grew and I found Ron Carpenter. What a profound man of God! A man with the mind of Christ who teaches from the heart. Then only did I start to understand what the difference was in the five-fold ministry and what an important role a teacher has.

My days were filled with Ron's messages – one series of sermons after another. I started to understand the importance of communion and of living holy and started using communion on a regular basis.

I started to repent for all the decisions I made from my flesh, and not seeking the wisdom of God or even consulting God on these matters. From financial, to leaving my home and walking into a home to live in sin, irrespective of the ring on my finger and trusting the word of man instead of the ways of God.

My career at that point was based in a Jewish cultured firm and I fully understood their ways as I was engulfed in this from my previous position of almost ten years.

Knowledge of the Jewish culture was the predestined attribute that ensured in me obtaining the current one. Through this I got to learn and understand the value of fasting. This now became my reality and very much a part of my current path.

The teachings I listened to started overlapping with my current reality as a Christian believer and follower of Jesus, with that of my daily Jewish culture at work, and I came to learn the merit of understanding how the feasts are recorded and practiced in my Bible and how some of these were still expected of us as believers today. Leviticus 23 describes these, in addition to the Sabbath as follows:

- Easter (Pesach/ Passover) – Through the crucifixion of Jesus Christ
- The Feast of First Fruits
- The Feast of Harvest
- The Day of Atonement

I would like to clarify at this point that I refer to us as believers. But quickly had to come to terms that there is a vast difference in being a believer in Jesus and being a follower of Jesus. For Satan is a believer in Jesus, but not a follower of Jesus. And I knew imminently that I wanted to be a follower of Jesus, not just a believer, but being a follower, meant that I needed to work at my relationship with Jesus. I am the one that was not standing in good stead. For the Word clearly states, that God changes not. He is the same yesterday, today and forever more. (Malachi 3:6).

This dedicated path meant change! It meant repentance, it meant not going back to old ways. Not just forgiveness, but true repentance in changed ways. I had to move beyond what I have always done, stop doing it and totally change direction and behavior.

Do you think this was taken kindly?

I now became the alien one, the one who is brainwashed, the one who has changed. Rightfully so, for reasons I could not and would not confess to a so-called believer, but not a follower of Christ. The one the Word refers to as a lukewarm believer. We no longer spoke the same language. The shift and the rift started and grew evidently wider.

I deepened the search for scripture, and it told me in Matthew 7:7–8 *"Ask, and it will be given to you. Seek, and you will find. Knock, and the door will be opened to you."*

Chapter 5
Presence and Confirmation

"The LORD is the one who will go before you. He will be with you; he will not leave you or abandon you. Do not be afraid or discouraged." – Deuteronomy 31:8

Silence does not mean absence.

Growing up as a child the concept of angels and angelic presence was not a strange phenomenon in my life and the lives of my parents. My father regularly had angelic presence and the ability to see and communicate in the spirit world. This brought great comfort at times.

After my divorce, I had the privilege of seeing and having angels in my home during a very difficult time. However, I did not have the ability or privilege to be able to communicate. I did, however, recognize the cognitive response of my body to higher fields of energy and the pre-descending smells of flowers that came with them. The light was over-powering bright and blue white with iridescence that cannot be described. The human eye is not trained to see in this glare. And the presence could only be acknowledged through intense electricity fields so to speak, and bright light observed through barely open eyes.

Both encounters but weeks apart brought comfort and peace. The understanding that my plight is very well seen, observed from above and the Father is working on my behalf. It was also in this period of my life that I could clearly hear the audible voice of God the Father in my left ear, calling me by my name. This was an undeniable reality.

At that time, my first point of call was my earthly father who knew of these things, and he confirmed that the voice is heard in the left ear. As his experience was similar and we discussed this in detail. Also, the latest angelic presence that he had and the conversation that took place.

I was privileged to be able to have this in my life.

After my divorce, I spent a holiday visiting my parents. It was customary for my mom to come into my bedroom at their home and tell me to get into bed with my dad, she is on her way with the morning coffee which we would all share together. Upon crawling in behind my dad's back, he immediately asked how I slept and if I was able to communicate with them.

Great was my astonishment that he knew of my visitors during the night! I asked him how he knew. He said that he woke up when he saw the bright lights approach the bedroom window and his first thought was that they were coming to visit him, but then he saw them enter through the wall at my bedroom window. He asked if I could manage to communicate this time. I confirmed.

I woke up during the night with the same energy vibrations all over my body and the smell of flowers. Immediately I switched to speaking in tongues and prayed over the fear. It subsided and I could open my eyes to the most glorious light. They were huge! They reached the ceiling, and their wings were vast. I could hear the singing, angel choir singing.

The only words that I could get out of my mouth at that point was: "What is going to happen to my son?" For the life of me I had no idea where that came from and was not something that I would ever think of asking. But it just came out.

The angels answered but in choir singing. The whole message was sung, and it was the same phrase over and over in the most beautiful audible words: "He will get his favor."

The sounds and the presence dissipated and left.

My father's additional confirmation of the presence brought clarity that this was not just my imagination or part of a dream. This was real, very, very real. My first experience in communicating with heavenly angels.

Many years after that, approximately five months before my father died, he phoned me in tears one morning. He wanted to know if the angels were with me the previous night. I said, "No" and asked concerning his emotional state.

He confirmed that God's voice audibly spoke to him during the night and said that He was coming to fetch him to take him home. And not only that, but that Dad should pack his suitcase and prepare. But more so, (which was the reason for the immense number of tears), was the fact that God said that He would fetch Dad first, then myself as now I was ready to go home, but Mom was not ready yet. And she would go last.

It took all my being to remain seemingly undisturbed during this immensely emotional discussion. I knew my father was ill and had dementia going on full blown Alzheimer's. But I also knew that I could never doubt his encounters with the Almighty. This by now had a clear track record.

A discussion followed on what the meaning was in "packing his suitcase and prepare" and I tried my best to console him that this was a wonderful message preparing him on what was to come, and he had the glorious gift of time, to say and to do what he deemed necessary or was unsaid in his life.

That I would go next was of great concern to him, and I refer to scripture here that led me to my explanation, that as the seed of my father, his faith covered me as a child and my salvation was ensured. Despite me being saved in my own right as a child of God. My mother, however, was not related to my father in terms of seed and it was her responsibility to take care of her own salvation. If the situation was turned around, and it was my mother who had the visit, the same principle would apply for me being of her seed as well. I refer to scripture.

1 Corinthians 7:14

"For the unbelieving husband is made holy by the wife, and the unbelieving wife is made holy by the husband. Otherwise, your children would be unclean, but as it is they are holy."

On 1 April 2019, my father went home to be with the Lord. This was the last discussed "visit" that I had with him.

I had not had any visitations since being in the "madhouse." I clearly understood that the environment was not conducive to what God wanted for me.

However, one evening after a very bad row and at the lowest of lows that I could possibly get, I was at the point of overdosing on medication. I sat at the edge of the bed, absolutely exasperated, and turned to swing my legs under the covers. I was flooded with emotion of hopelessness and the will to no longer live.

The vibrations started.

And I knew I wasn't alone.

God did not forget about me.

He sent His angel to appear by my side.

"For he will give his angels orders concerning you, to protect you in all your ways. They will support you with their hands so that you will not strike your foot against a stone." –

Psalm 91:11–12.

There was no communication, just presence.

I put the tablets down and turned over to sleep, a deep restful sleep.

Chapter 6
The Mind of Christ

"Therefore, brothers and sisters, in view of the mercies of God, I urge you to present your bodies as living sacrifice, holy and pleasing to God; this is your true worship. Do not be conformed to this age, but be transformed by the renewing of your mind, so that you may discern what is the good, pleasing, and perfect will of God." – Romans 12: 1–2

Renewing the mind results in personal transformation!

When the mind has changed, the life will follow.

It is literal.

It is actual.

It is sure.

It is for everyone.

There are three levels to God's will, the good, the acceptable and the perfect will of God. There is no case that is too far gone. There is nothing that is too hard for the Lord. What you grab hold of in faith is contingent on how renewed your mind is!

If you become like a dog with a bone; adamant that nothing will move you – be sure the victory will come! It is crucial that you wash your mind daily in the Word of God. It is alive and active!

The Word of God is likened unto water that can wash and cleanse your mind. (Ephesians 5:26) As you read and speak it, circumstances will change and happen.

"When we make a committed decision to change, we switch roles from slave to master." – Steve Wharton. In biblical terms from victim to victor.

My new reality was embracing the change that came with the renewed mind. I had to come to terms with the obedience in Christ and if that is what it took in every way or form to move me out, then that is what I would do. The decision was made.

All fresh hell broke loose!

My body was now a "no go" zone, I fasted regularly, took communion every day and understood that my faith muscles are being built and strengthened. I was going to be obedient as it became very evident that obedience was key to moving forward. (Ephesians 4:20–24)

If I had to paint a mental picture at this point, it would be the analogy of a waterpipe. I understood that if that pipe is rusted, blocked and dirty on the inside, it could not facilitate the smooth flow of water or produce clear clean water for that matter. Similarly, God needs clean vessels for the Holy Spirit to do its work.

I ploughed through scriptures and poured over the examples of obedience. Obedience became my obsession as I understood that when you loved God, you would be obedient in observing his ways. This is clearly set out in Deuteronomy 28.

It became evident that a man that leads a woman away from God into sin, is not a man of God, but a man of earthly habits who adheres to the lusts of the flesh. I was caught in the web of an insatiable lust of the flesh, which could never be satisfied. (Ephesians 4: 17–20)

The enemy used the open door of pornography to run rampant in the "madhouse" with the desires of the flesh, the obsession of self and consistent attention seeking. The picture slowly started to reveal truth, the more I listened and searched scripture.

Through this I came to learn about the Prayer of Petition. Also, the concept of sowing seed (offering) into the ministry where you are fed, towards the Prayer of Petition, naming your seed and then praying over that seed. Regularly keeping it in God's remembrance as He says in His Word about praying His promises back to Him. I touch on this later but share here my first Prayer of Petition on 17 February 2021.

Dear Abba Father,

In Your word it is written in **Isaiah 55:11**:

"So is my word that goes out from my mouth; it will not return to me empty, but will accomplish what I desire and achieve the purpose for which I sent it."

In Your word it is written in **John 10:10**:

"The thief comes only to steal, kill and destroy; I have come that they may have life and have it to the full."

And in **Proverbs 6:31**:

"Yet if he is caught, he must pay sevenfold, though it costs him all the wealth of his house."

Lord, I bring the following before you:

1. I repent again on the fact that I have signed surety to a vast and detrimental extent for my son for both their vehicles, the insurance for one (although this is diligently paid for), the cellphone and the revolving credit loan.

2. I repent Abba Father for the bad stewardship of the credit card and overdraft – which was partly due to the non-payment of my son's responsibilities. I repent Father that I did not trust and seek You on these matters.

3. Father, I further repent for moving in with this man without consulting with you as well. I trusted the word of man (which was already broken after one promise) against my better judgement.

4. Father, I seem to consistently ask for forgiveness for having to sacrifice my body for a roof over my head. I have prayed so many times for this Lord, and you know my heart.

Father, today I pray in the light of the above scriptures that You in Your might, majesty and wisdom collect the debt for me sevenfold as is written in the above scriptures that the enemy return to me:

a. The peace that surpasses all understanding, that was stolen from me in that, when getting home at night and not having to sacrifice my body for a roof over my head in sex before marriage.

b. For all the broken promises and lies spoken to me about having a home of my own.

c. For all the broken promises and lies of marriage.

d. For the continued deceit of demon influence of lust and perversion which entered and found a foothold in him through pornography and the like.

e. For all the time that was lost in trying to make You count and failing.

f. For all the time that was lost in effort to living a fruitful, joyful life in You and not continuously in battle.

g. For all the money that was spent on the house, in effort to make it a home.

h. For all the money that was handed out in time, effort, talking and pleading with the children to pay their responsibilities.

i. For all the time spent in worry and trying to make plans to make it right financially and emotionally.

j. For all the emotional abuse and lies and verbal

destruction of the enemy towards me through him.

k. For all the injustice that I had to live through and continuously had to be chased away because of manipulation and control.

l. For all the destruction as a person in effort to make me what I am not, through their music, drinking, socializing, discussion and belittling me behind my back.

I praise You Lord, that You know what is good, what is just, what is righteous and what is worthy. I praise You Lord that You are bigger than all the above and that You are the God of the impossible and that You go before me to make the crooked places straight.

I praise You Lord and lift Your name up High for the comfort of this message and that You will honor Your word and that it will not return void. In the mighty unmatched name of Jesus Christ.

Amen.

Prayers of Petition, writing them, dating, and signing them proceeded with sowing into them. This became my lifestyle, together with intermittent fasting and taking communion.

During this time, I started listening to the services of Dr. Jolynne Whittaker. Prophetic ministry was now being revealed to me and I reveled in the understanding that once God places you under or in touch with the prophetic, change is about to happen. I remained and stood, pressed in, and prayed. I continued my study of the scriptures in tandem with the prophetic and revelation upon revelation was provided.

Do not be deceived, times were all but pleasant. Matters get worse before they get better, and this was no different.

One evening, very despondent I lowered by head in prayer

and poured my heart out. During prayer when I kept silent, there was an unction in my spirit and the word: "Stand." I prayed further and kept silent again. The words louder, almost an urgent command, in my ear this time came: "You Stand!" I did not imagine it and my eyes flew open. That wasn't part of my prayer! But it was an answer.

I share with you here the second Prayer of Petition dated 24 February 2021:

Dearest Abba Father, Jesus and Holy Spirit,

This morning, I lift praises and sing Halleluja to Your Majesty and glory! Abba Lord, no one can be equaled to You or Your works. Lord, I stand humbled as I listened to Your great works and the manifestation of visitations – how wonderful to hear angels sing in the morning.

Father, I praise and thank You for the lovely word and prophetic utterances I receive and hear. Thank you for the teachings – only You know what I need and what is required for my inner growth and restoration! I praise You Lord!

Father, it is written in **Psalm 37:3–4***:*

3 "Trust in the LORD and do what is good; dwell in the land and live securely.

4 Take delight in the LORD and he will give you your heart's desires."

Dearest Jehovah Jireh, You are my provider in all things, my Redeemer and my Rock. Lord, I come humbly before You this morning with my request and desires of my heart. You say in Your Word Lord that I am to write down the plan and to make it plain.

My request this morning, in the mighty name of Jesus is for my own home, a home for Mom and sufficient funds to provide for both homes and to take care of Mom in her financial and physical requirements. The plan is written out as per my statement on the opposite page. Lord, I am trusting You for a supernatural blessing for this, as there is no way I can do this on my own in any manner or form!

Your word says in **Romans 13:8**:

"Do not owe anyone anything, except to love one another, for the one who loves another has fulfilled the law."

Also, it says in **Jeremiah 29:11**:

"For I know the plans I have for you" – this is the Lord's declaration – "plans for your well-being, not for disaster, to give you a future and a hope."

And **Philippians 4:19**:

"And my God will supply all your needs according to his riches in glory in Christ Jesus."

Father, I can only do this with Your blessing, guidance and the wisdom that only You can provide.

I feel compelled to take care of Mom as You very well know Lord. She has done so much for me in my life and continues doing so in her unique way. Your word says in **Acts 20:35**:

"In every way I've shown you that it is necessary to help the weak by laboring like this and to remember the words of the Lord Jesus, because he said, "It is more blessed to give than to receive."

Proverbs 27:23:

"Know well the condition of your flock, and pay attention to your herds,"

Adonai, not only is it my heart's desire to give Mom a home, a haven and safe place of her own with the comfort and care that she is worthy of, but also my deep heart's desire to own my own home on this earth Lord. I truly repent of my wrong decisions in resulting where I live now. Your word promises in **Amos 9:13–15**:

13 "Look the days are coming – this is the LORD's

declaration – when the plowman will overtake the reaper and the one who treads grapes, the sower of seed. The mountains will drip with sweet wine, and all the hills will flow with it.

14 I will restore the fortunes of my people Israel. They will rebuild and occupy ruined cities, plant vineyards and drink their wine, make gardens and eat their produce.

15 I will plant them on their land, and they will never again be uprooted from the land I have given them. The LORD your God has spoken"

Oh, how I stand on this promise, Lord! How glorious it would be to have this manifest in our lives! And all the glory will be Yours, dear Lord.

Dearest Abba Father, there is no possible way that I can make this happen on my own. My trust I place completely in You, Elohim – this is a Supernatural miracle request. But I praise You, El Olam that nothing is impossible with You and that You are no man that You can lie. For it is written in **Ephesians 3:20**:

"Now to him who is able to do above and beyond all that we ask or think according to the power that works in us"

I thank you Yahweh that it is written in **Deuteronomy 28:12:**

"The LORD will open for you his abundant storehouse, the sky, to give your land rain in its season and to bless all the work of your hands. You will lend to many nations, but you will not borrow"

Proverbs 10:22

"The LORD's blessing enriches, and he adds no painful effort to it."

And truly have You blessed me El Shaddai, in my coming in and my going out! I praise You Lord for blessing me indeed!

Psalm 84:11:

"For the LORD God is a sun and shield. The LORD grants favor and honor; he does not withhold the good from those who *live with integrity."*

Dear Jehovah Raah, I pray your guidance and wisdom as per James 1:5 to stand, withstand the guiles of the evil one, and do what is right in Your eyes oh Lord. I pray for supernatural growth, and the expansion of my tent to encompass ALL You have for me Jesus. I lift Your name up high for the promises I can stand on.

Hallelujah to You El Shaddai! Hallelujah!
Matthew 21:22
"And if you believe, you will receive whatever you ask for in prayer."

Amen, Amen and Amen! I thank you for this inheritance of Matthew 21:22 from You Jehovah Jireh and as an inheritance from my earthly father.

I can only humbly say thank you, thank you and thank you. Bless You oh God, in the name of Jesus.
I love you, Lord!

I share these prayers as examples of my journey and my Prayers of Petition at the time of seeking truth and manifesting God's promises in my life. I encourage you to seek scripture and write your own Prayers of Petition, date and sign them, sow into them and watch what God does. I will speak about this in the coming chapters.

During this period, I made it my business to find out more about seed time and harvest time. Working through the teachings of Neal Reyes online, who does great work on teaching Kingdom principles such as the Tithe, First Fruit Offering, Seed time and Harvest time, Guarding your Soul Gates, The Importance of Partnership and Kingdom Financial Principles. I would like to encourage you to take the time to study these and take notes which you can reflect on. This increased my awareness of the mechanics of the Kingdom.

On 25 February 2021, I made an intentional choice of resisting evil by starting with a Fast of Ester.

A fast of obedience, in obedience for clearer revelation on the way forward.

To understand the significance of this fast, please read the book of Esther and how God worked His hand in these uncanny circumstances.

Chapter 7
The Fast of Esther

"Go and assemble all the Jews who can be found in Susa and fast for me. Don't eat or drink for three days, night or day. I and my female servants will also fast in the same way. After that, I will go to the king even if it is against the law. If I perish, I perish." – Esther 4:16

The fast for protection from the evil one. Obtaining deliverance and direction from God.

Fasting is a biblical way to truly humble oneself in the sight of God. The same way we must feed and nourish our physical body to grow, we must do the same with our spiritual body, for our spiritual growth.

There is power in fasting:
- Fasting will bring deliverance.
- The will of God will be revealed.
- Unbelief will be removed from our mind.
- We obtain power over circumstances.
- It will bring deliverance from troubles, worries, needs and spiritual conflict.
- It is the cleansing of your soul.
- It transforms your prayer life into a richer and more personal experience.
- It results in renewed faith.

It is important to understand that you need to have a clear objective when wanting to fast. And that this objective be taken to God in prayer. My objectives in this fast were for the following:
- The grace to handle an impossible situation.
- For spiritual strength.
- For Divine intervention.

When you do make the decision to embark on this fast, please read the book of Esther and take your circumstances to God. It is vitally important that you prepare yourself spiritually for the fast and that you fast in expectancy of solutions and a way forward. (Hebrews 11:6)

During the process of the fast, confess every sin the Holy Spirit calls to your remembrance and ask God's forgiveness (1 John 1:9). Make restitution as the Holy Spirit leads you.

Surrender your life fully to Jesus Christ; refuse to obey your worldly nature (Romans 12:1–2).

Meditate on God's attributes (Psalm 38:9–10; 103:1–8. 11–13).

Please be very clear that fasting is pushing back the plate and denying the flesh to enable hearing and growing in the spirit. Fasting is not denying yourself from technology, cellphones, television and the like. That is false doctrine. Fasting is denying yourself food, and only drinking water. That is called an absolute fast.

Furthermore, if you have never fasted before, please note that fasting is a muscle that needs to be developed. A full fast can be started off with one day at a time and as you progress and get stronger you would want to increase your fasting time to three days at a time, dependent on the type of fast you wish to do.

I refer you to scripture where certain matters can only be

dealt with by prayer, supplication to God and fasting. Fasting is mentioned over seventy times in scripture. Through many examples of people in the Bible who fasted, we can know that God grants supernatural revelation and wisdom through this practice. Moses, Daniel and even Jesus fasted! Scripture tells us that fasting will help us grow a more intimate relationship with Christ and will open our eyes to what He wants to teach us.

Joel 2: 12 – 13

12 "Even now – this is the LORD's declaration – turn to me with all your heart, with fasting, weeping, and mourning.

13 Tear your hearts, not just your clothes, and return to the LORD your God. For he is gracious and compassionate, slow to anger, abounding in faithful love, and he relents from sending disaster."

What a word!

During this fast, the Holy Spirit led me to make the decision to do the twenty-one-day Daniel fast. I could only assume that there was to be more for me to understand and obtain than in an absolute fast over a longer period.

A first for me ever!

Chapter 8
The Daniel Fast – For Breakthrough and Change

"As for you, Solomon my son, know the god of your father, and serve him wholeheartedly and with a willing mind, for the Lord searches every heart and understands the intention of every thought. If you seek him, he will be found by you, but if you abandon him, he will reject you forever." – 1 Chronicles 28:9

Eating to purify the body, edify the soul and open the heart.

It took time to research and learn the truth and ways of the Daniel Fast. Spending time on the internet and getting the information together was one of the most fulfilling experiences I went through. I worked out weekly menus for the three weeks, made shopping lists, downloaded recipes, and got my act together to prepare what was required. Due to the nature of my work, I was in the habit of preparing meals and ensuring that the fridge was stocked over a weekend. This eliminated any running around or having to do a shopping trip during the week and spend unnecessary money on items that might not be required.

This was one of the few times that I had fun preparing for and it gave me great joy. I couldn't explain why. Today, I can reflect on this and can only attribute it to the fact that the soul knew change was coming.

I was astonished to find so many good and healthy options

that I could eat and prepare to ensure that the meals were balanced and that a good healthy plate of food with vegetables, salads and permissible ingredients could be so filling.

The fast started on 1 March 2021.

This time was fraught with temptation and ridicule! How I have changed, have I now become a vegan, what's wrong with me and I am living in my own world.

For me to write the words – it was tough – here on a piece of paper, is the understatement of the world.

The instruction came in **Psalm 1:1–3**

1 "How happy is the one who does not walk in the advice of the wicked or stand in the pathway with sinners or sit in the company of mockers!"

2 "Instead, his delight is in the LORD's instruction, and he meditates on it day and night."

3 "He is like a tree planted beside flowing streams that bears its fruit in its season and whose leaf does not wither. Whatever he does prospers."

The time had come to distance myself from the whole family, children, and him. Not attending get-togethers with the excessive drinking. No sharing of information. This included deleting and blocking every family member, including him from all social media whatsoever.

I couldn't afford the association. Please understand that God will bring you to a point in your life where you need to clean "house." There will be people in your life who cannot go where you are going.

You can still love them from a distance, but your journey and your elevation does not include everybody in your life. Your actions will be misconstrued and not understood. That is part of the journey.

This caused its own kind of "devil dance" in the doorway!

During this period, I was the healthiest that I had ever been in my life! I even lost weight and I felt good. My spirit muscles were gaining strength and my daily emotions were slowly stabilizing within me. I found inner peace which I could not explain.

I distanced myself from everyone and cut off all communications and ties in any form or manner. I had to start saving myself from emotional murder.

I would, however, be tormented with loud music and the usual drink in hand when he would braai on his own and sing at the top of his voice in spite, to provoke me. This would be followed by days of the silent treatment.

It was during one of these periods of silent treatment that the wi-fi was installed at the "madhouse." I was not informed and saw this almost three days after installation. Upon making mention of this and if there was any intention of providing the password of the system, I was told that he would have, but I was the one not speaking to him. Yeah right – and when was that going to be? At the rapture when he realized where I was there ain't no signal?

It took all the willpower I could muster up to close the bedroom door, put earphones on and retreat to the secret place with God. I would then listen to a sermon to find encouragement.

Jerry Savelle and Jesse Duplantis were but two of the online pastors that I thoroughly enjoyed listening to – purely because not only are they friends and very successful in their own right – they had the most amazing sense of humor! I needed to laugh again. I haven't laughed in such a very long time. I needed to find the joy of absolute inner laughter and fun.

Jesse taught and spoke on his interactions with God and his conversations with Him, his visit to heaven and how this relationship was reality and was fun. I instantly knew that I wanted it – and I wanted it big time! And then he started talking about visitations to Heaven and a new kind of excitement took hold of me. I want to visit Heaven!

Come now, let's get real – you think I can discuss this with anyone? The only one that really shared my journey was my mom and one good friend. The isolation with myself continued, my search deepened, and my journey became more intense and dedicated.

I craved freedom, I wanted out and I needed to find the way, the how and the funds. The unction in my spirit was that of a bird wanting to flee a cage.

My life started to turn into making plans, thinking, and dreaming. The night-time dreams during sleep became more vivid and I started a dream journal, trying to make sense of it all and going to scripture. Finding significance in the dream journey and the messages I was shown. I will cover this in an ensuing chapter.

My mind started focusing forward and detaching from the present.

Chapter 9
Dreaming the Dreams

"And it will be in the last days, says God, that I will pour out my Spirit on all people; then your sons and your daughters will prophesy, your young men will see visions, and your old men will dream dreams." – Acts 2:17

Understanding the pictures, brings hope!

Dreams are a natural phenomenon of our lives, one that is mostly underrated and scoffed at and contributed to having too much pizza or cheese the previous evening! No doubt there are some that could be classified as such.

But as a follower of Jesus, you will soon identify the difference. God dreams are prophetic, clear and you remember them vividly.

I was advised through a sermon I listened to, to keep a journal of my dreams and in the process, you would then be able to go back and distinguish certain incidents or even items that would appear in future dreams and would instinctively know the gist of the dream. This was a muscle that I had to develop and understand in my own life.

Journaling your dreams is a very personal walk. It takes time, practice, and dedication. It takes understanding of your dream within the context of your life, your decrees, Prayers of Petition and your daily quiet time prayers.

Dreams have a lot to do with the condition of your heart posture in faith and your path. Your prayer journal will not make any sense whatsoever to any outsider or even anyone in your household for that matter, as it's not supposed to. It is your personal journey and path, unique to your circumstances in that period of your life.

I deemed it important to share with you at this juncture one of the most vivid and important dreams that made me understand that my path had reached breakthrough point. As fear-filled and horrifying as it was it was in one word: – **Freedom!**

This was the dream on the first night of the Daniel Fast.

The dream started out with me entering a large castle-like building where great preparations were at hand for a wedding feast to take place. I was going from hall to hall looking at the preparations and décor. My adult children were in the background, being happy and in good spirits. I was enticed and taken by the preparations.

The next moment, I heard the hissing sound, and everybody started running. I stood. The giant python entered that specific hall. It was so huge its body filled the banquet hall and its head lifted, the size of I would say, at least four bulldog heads together. The eyes were bloodshot and the animosity and violent state very evident. The scales on its face were black green in color. It came closer and the tongue started to flick. I could feel the warmth of its breath close to my face.

By supernatural strength, I lifted my arms, launched, and grabbed hold of its mouth and I squeezed with all my might keeping it shut! I screamed victory and held on for dear life. I knew I'd won.

I was told that I screamed out loud and woke him in the next room. My immediate revelation was that of victory and that I have overcome the enemy! At last! I have shut the mouth of the evil one.

On reading later that day, I found the following descriptions and explanations, which I share. These are from the dream dictionary by Apostle JP Bekker who pastors a church in Pretoria, with several campuses across South Africa. A man for whom I have great respect and deposited revelations that were instrumental on my faith path.

Python:

A large demonic stronghold that crushes and opposes breakthrough, stopping you short of entering into enlargement, it co-labors with Jezebel to steal inheritance and increase, causes divination or witchcraft.

Refer to: Leviticus 20:27

Deuteronomy 18:11

1 Chronicles 19:13

I could almost dance the jig right there! For the first time I had a taste of victory, and it was good!

The dreams continued for eleven nights in a row.

Dream 2:

I dreamt of a house on the rocks with beautiful lawns in between. The place was sheltered. The message was clear – *I was building my house on the Rock.*

Dream 3:

A sniper was shooting at me, all dressed in black from top to toe, with a rifle. I walked up to him and bent the rifle upwards with my left hand and hit the man over the head with a stick in my right hand.

The message – *I was overcoming the enemy attacks.*

Dream 4:

I was holding and cuddling a lamb.

The message – *I was embracing Jesus.*

Dream 5:

I was doing laundry and clean water was being hosed everywhere. And there was a bowl of strawberries.

The message – *I was being purified and a rebirth was taking place.*

Dream 6:

I was cleaning out a defecated toilet and I was also eating green leaves.

The message – *This was the end of a crappy season, and I am moving in the truth of the Word.*

Dream 7:

I dreamt of down syndrome children. (In my reality there was down syndrome individuals in our family and this matter was always close to my heart). I could not however, fathom the meaning of this dream to date.

Dream 8:

I was flying through space, breaking supernaturally through "chicken wire" boundaries.

The message – *There would be new situations, new thinking, and experiences which I have never had before – a breaking of barriers. I needed to get ready to experience something I have never experienced before.*

The second part of the dream was that I was baking a pie and there were new tastes in it.

The message – *Baking is about making changes. I was feeling ready for a new location and a new me.*

Dream 9:

I was in a busy market with my mom. We had glasses of champagne in our hands, but the contents of my purse was stolen.

The message – *The busy market was a sign of prosperity,*

coming into a new job, financial improvements, and significant help. The champagne was the sign of celebrations on the way. The stolen contents of my purse were, that my identity had been stolen.

Dream 10:
I dreamt of a new custom-made vehicle for me.
The message – *There was a new way for me, a life unique to me.*

The second part of the dream involved animals charging back and forth:

Lynx – *this meant enemies and false friends.*

Leopards – *this meant fearless attitude. With great speed I can avoid complicated situations.*

Lions – *Bravery, strength, courage, and protection would be mine.*

Elephant family breaking through the fence – *invincible, thick-skinned, sin not dealt with.*

A baby which I had to name Samsara! – *prosperity, a new beginning the rebirth and restoration of my soul.*

The third part of the dream:
A small baby with faeces pouring out of the nappy all over me.
The message – *My hard work will pay off!*

Dream 11:
I was building a large wooden desk of wood!
The message – *A new career or job*

Are you excited yet?
I now understood why the Daniel Fast had to take place and that my mind and soul had to be receptive for the download of the messages. Overwhelmed is an understatement to describe my

feelings about the absolute goodness of God!

The significance of this time will always remain with me as the biggest tangible change of direction in my life.

But it was a choice.

A choice to sit at the feet of Jesus.

A choice to set myself apart – irrespective of how hard that was.

A choice to live, move and have my being in Christ.

A choice to rise.

Chapter 10
The Anatomy of Breakthrough

"From the days of John the Baptist until now, the kingdom of heaven has been suffering violence, and the violent have been seizing it by force." – Matthew 11:12

If you fail to recognize, you cannot receive!

Breakthrough requires your faith and your participation. You must lay hold of your breakthrough. Dream it, speak it, work it (even though you can't see it *yet*) and visualize it. Once you recognize the value, you will lay hold of it.

Breakthrough is always preceded by difficulty and limitations. There is tremendous travail and pain! Equate this to the process of giving birth. Once that new life is born, there is no remembrance of the pain. But the pain must be endured to birth that new life, to build muscle and endurance.

1. *Suddenly*

All breakthroughs are supernatural! They always happen suddenly.

Acts 2:2

"Suddenly a sound like that of a violent rushing wind came from heaven, and it filled the whole house where they were staying."

We serve a magnificent God, who does the impossible, in an

improbable way, to achieve impeccable impact for us, His imperfect people! And he does it suddenly. But we must stand in faith, and in full expectation of the miracle.

2. Remain positive and God connected
Cynicism will always neutralize your suddenly. Don't be negative! And please hear me – don't take a break from the things of God. Stand irrespective, for your breakthrough.

3. Create the right environment
You must create the right environment internally and externally to receive. The attitude of expectancy is the atmosphere for miracles. You need to create the right environment. Hang around faithful people.

Remember the scripture where Jesus could not do miracles in His hometown? For they did not receive it. They could not perceive Him as the Messiah, therefore they could not receive.

Mark 6:4
'A prophet is not without honor except in his hometown, among his relatives, and in his household."

Your breakthrough will bring discomfort to the people around you.

4. How to activate the Breaker Anointing
I address anointing and the process in later chapters in more depth. In this section I speak about anointing for the breakthrough specifically.

1 John 2:27
"As for you, the anointing remains in you, and you don't need anyone to teach you. Instead, his anointing teaches you about all things and is true and is not a lie; just as it has taught

you, remain in him."

Philippians 4:13

"I am able to do all things through him who strengthens me."

The word "Christ" means the anointed one. He received the anointing. He is the Messiah, the Breaker that has already gone before you. We are dealing with the one who breaks forward and makes a way. The anointing is supernatural equipment to do the job. In Luke 4:18–19, Jesus identifies Himself as the breaker!

Chrio in Greek means to smear or to rub oil (Anoint). The heavenly oil that, once activated, releases supernatural power!

When this oil is on you, you overcome things and receive supernatural results. If you make your vessel available, the oil will flow! Do you remember the story of the widow and her sons that had to bring all the empty vessels into the house and God blessed her and the oil just kept coming. But the moment there was no more empty vessels, the oil stopped flowing.

Your availability is the *key* to releasing the anointing. Whatever you do not recognize you do not release! So please, get hold of this impactful truth to enable it in your life. Learn how to recognize the value of the anointing on your life.

Whatever you steward well will become more and if appreciated, will increase in value. The oil that you have will determine the capacity you can receive.

Action activates the anointing!

Open your mouth and speak. When you don't place a demand on the anointing it will not manifest. Much demonstration of the anointing needs much demand on it.

Break through, break forth and break out!

1 Corinthians 1:27

"Instead, God has chosen what is foolish in the world to

shame the wise, and God has chosen what is weak in the world to shame the strong."

You immediately recall the saying of don't despise humble beginnings.

To save the world, God sent us a baby boy. When He wanted to save the Israelites out of bondage, He sent a shepherd, David. God hides himself in simplicity! He uses oil as His power.

Do you now understand the importance of making yourself available for the anointing to flow through you? The anointing causes you to rise above limitations. Read about the anointing that came upon Hannah in 1 Samuel 1:8 – 20.

For every limitation there is an anointing to overcome that specific limitation. You must understand this. The anointing makes you different, it sets you apart. You will see a different result than the rest. But it means that you need to set yourself apart from the rest.

If you *want* to live like no one else – you *must* live like no one else!

When you come to the end of yourself, the oil is being crushed. In the Garden of Gethsemane (means olive press), Jesus asked that if at all possible the cup pass Him by. This was an intense period of crushing! Unless the olive is crushed the oil cannot be released. See this.

In summary, this is a process of emptying of self, where God fills you and you go beyond your natural limitations!

It was the same with the Israelites when they reached the wall of Jericho. They could not defeat this on their own. But by the power of God, the Jericho walls came down.

5. <u>What does it mean to operate in the anointing?</u>

Every single person must come to a crossroads in their life, a defining moment where you realize who you are and what you have received. When you realize your own insufficiency and your own incapacity, you can now be positioned to rely on the capacity of God.

The anointing releases the capacity of God in you, so that you can begin to function in the God filled life.

Numbers 22:21-38 speaks about the story of the incident with Balaam and his donkey. Sometimes God must use the donkeys in our lives to speak for us. You cannot curse what God has blessed.

Not only is the anointing powerful, but it is also both tangible and transferable.

Chapter 11
Identity

"For God has not given us a spirit of fear, but one of power, love, and sound judgment (mind)" – 2 Timothy 1:7

Using the power you were given.

After the previous chapter and being told that my identity was stolen, I had to make work of addressing this within the Daniel Fast period.

When captive in a situation where you are consistently told that you are mad, bipolar and the nightmare of two psychologists, it is human nature to cringe and doubt your worth in existence. It was only within the Daniel Fast that I could take my power back and decree that I am of sound mind.

It is God who designed your purpose and your identity. He has a plan for your life and knows your end from your beginning. (Jeremiah 1:5) There is a book in heaven about you. Your life has been planned and mapped out by your Creator. (Jeremiah 29:11) It is crucial that you get back to the root of who you are in the Word of God. Your identity comes from God.

God can help you get up, speed up and get you back on track. But you need to get out of the memory lane and the melancholy mindset. That is a trap of the evil one. You are precious to God. You are His workmanship. He has plans for you. A plan for hope and a future to an expected end.

Research took me to **Matthew 6: 19–21**

19 "Don't store up for yourselves treasures on earth, where moth and rust destroy and where thieves break in and steal.

20 But store up for yourselves treasures in heaven, where neither moth nor rust destroys, and where thieves don't break in and steal.

21 For where your treasure is, there your heart will be also."

I clearly understood that my identity is in Christ, that I came from God and that I am who He says I am. My worth lies in what He made me. According to scripture, I am beautifully and wonderfully made, and my focus is heavenward, homeward to where my Father is. I came into the knowledge and being of whose child I am. What He sees not only of me but in me.

But I also got a clear picture that this identity that I have been given by Jesus has been tarnished and destroyed, stolen, and murdered. I had become a person walking in fear, treading on eggshells and pushed into a corner.

I had head knowledge, but I needed to put that into practice! How do I do that?

My conversations and search also revealed narcissistic traits, one being that narcissists isolate their victims, and tell their victims lies about what their friends think about them. Deliberately misinterpreting conversations to give the impression that your friends confided in them. Then turning around and saying that he would not reveal the name of the person as I would confront them. To ensure the misconstrued truth would not be revealed.

The goal – to paint a so-called picture of who I am for the world to see, which is contrary to what God says I am. The tactics became more evident, and I realized that I was becoming a person

I didn't like. I was stripped of being a woman, of my femininity, stripped of the image that God says in His Word and His description of me.

I had to overcome the fear and reinstate my power! I had to see the serpent for who he was and acknowledge that the lies and deception were one of the greatest weapons used against me.

I went back to scripture – **Proverbs 15:4**

"The tongue that heals is a tree of life, but a devious tongue breaks the spirit."

A sermon of Dr. Jolynne Whittaker guided me to speak, to shout, if need be, that which I wanted to see. If a devious tongue could break the spirit, what did I have to say that would empower me and move me forward?

Job 22:28 (NKJV)

"You will also declare a thing, and it will be established for you; so light will shine on your ways."

From my Prayers of Petition, I understood that praying God's promises to Him would result in the manifestation of my heart's desires. Now I could speak my future into tangible existence, backed by scripture and I could change my life.

I wrote them down and memorized scripture to anchor my words. Every morning, the moment I got into my car to drive to work I would say my decrees and I share them here gladly, for they changed my life:

I am the daughter of the highest God.

I walk in freedom, love, and power.

My body is healthy, my mind is sound, and my vision is 20/20.

My life is going upwards, onwards, and forwards, spiritually, and physically.

No weapon formed against me will prosper and every tongue

that rises up against me I will condemn, for I have been given authority to trample on snakes and scorpions and no harm shall come nigh me.

For though a thousand fall by my left and ten thousand by my right no pestilence shall come nigh my house.

For me and my house, we serve the Lord.

My new home is manifesting, fully paid for, peaceful and a place of rest. For it is written that the children of the Lord shall live in peaceful habitations, places of undisturbed rest and peace.

My new job, a high echelon position is manifesting, it will pay me the salary I require in the mighty name of Jesus.

I decree and declare that my debt is settled and fully paid up in the name of Jesus.

Together with these decrees, I downloaded worship music and played this every morning in my car after saying my decrees and started singing on the way to work. It happened involuntarily.

I knew from the teachings of Neal Reyes, that worship was a cardinal weapon against the enemy, and I was determined to use everything I possibly could. I developed a bulldog tenacity and wouldn't budge for no one, least of all the enemy.

Please understand that everything in life has protocol. It takes a certain protocol to enter a room and a protocol to remain in that room. The faith walk is no different. The protocol for the faith walk is obedience. It is not negotiable.

God will meet you on the fertile ground of your obedience and bring opportunities to you. (Isaiah 22:22) Stay connected to the vine!

Psalms 75:6–7

6 "Exaltation does not come from the east, the west, or the desert.

7 for God is the Judge: He brings down one and exalts

another."

Needless to say, my prayer journal and notes were read by him at some point and resulted in ridicule. I knew this was born out of a place of absolute ignorance and secular thinking. There was no point in trying to explain the contrary.

Sadly, I realized that anything I read, listened to, and made notes about was best kept with me wherever I go. And most of my books and journals stored at the office.

A walk of faith is very often a lonely one. Not one that is understood by many. Your journey is unique to you and your calling too. Not all are called to preach, prophesy, teach or write. But we all have greatness in us to share, build-up and help. Also know that it is, I call it the "stealth" of God to develop who he chooses in the dark. His methods are controversial to that which man might choose or deliberate.

I, by now had the revelation that faith without work is dead. That "work' meant to diligently seek, search, learn and practice. To grow your faith so you can walk in it. For God placed whatever we require within us. It is for us to develop those muscles, recognize the talent and make it work for us. The picture was starting to reveal itself and the walk became clear.

It still wasn't an easy road, far from it. But it now became a manageable one, a one of focus, of standing, speaking, and closing my eyes to that which threatened to inundate my pure existence.

The change was not only happening in my personal life, but the spill-over was now also in my work life as well.

Was I so blind? Is it truly a case of there is no eye so blind as those who don't want to see?

Chapter 12
Opposing Evil – Standing against Attacks of the Enemy

"For our struggle is not against flesh and blood, but against the rulers, against the authorities, against the cosmic powers of this darkness, against evil, spiritual forces in the heavens.: –
Ephesians 6:12

Understand that the evil one uses people to deceive and lie!

It is crucial to spend time in the Word to grow! Also be careful who you give access to. The Father will reveal to you who needs to have access to you – ask Him. Guard your heart. You will obtain wisdom and have favor with God. Your standing in faith pleases God. (Luke 2:52)

The Lord will then surround you with favor and bless you. You will have angelic protection. (Hebrews 1:14)

Then put on the full armor of God, to be protected, so the arrows and darts of the enemy cannot penetrate. **Ephesians 6:14–18** says:

14 "Stand, therefore, with truth like a belt around your waist, righteousness like armor on your chest,

15 and your feet sandaled with readiness for the gospel of peace.

16 In every situation take up the shield of faith with which you can extinguish all the flaming arrows of the evil one.

17 Take the helmet of salvation and the sword of the Spirit – which is the word of God.

18 Pray at all times in the Spirit with every prayer and request and stay alert with all perseverance and intercession for all the saints."

God requires boldness and bravery from us. Paul describes the Christian journey as a battle. No matter how strong or courageous you are, there are moments in your life that you find yourself in overwhelming situations. Paul says if you are going to defeat the devil you must use the armor of God.

I want to take some time and address each of these aspects here for you to have a better understanding of how to apply these and why.

1. *"With truth like a belt" (a girdle)*

The Roman soldiers wore a tunic. In order to keep this tunic from getting in their way, they wore a girdle (a belt). This girdle would be worn around the waist to tie everything together.

Now, in the Christian life our girdle or belt is that of truth. And the belt of truth is the truth of the Word of God over our lives. When we wake up in the morning, the first thing that we need to reach for is the Word of God and let the Word of God get into our lives. Truth is what gives our armor security and strength.

The god of this world is the father of lies, and you are living on this earth as a child of God. It is imperative that you put on the girdle of truth each and every day. If we are questioning God's Word or not apply it, then Satan is going to get the victory. The belt of truth means the application of truth to my and your life.

Satan is the liar, and if my loins are not girded with truth, I am going to believe his lie. It is important that we immerse ourselves in scripture and we apply the truth in our lives.

2. *"Righteousness like armor on your chest"*

The breastplate of righteousness is for the front and the back, which protects all the vital organs in the heat of the battle. The righteousness is not our righteousness but God's. **Isaiah 64:6** says *"All of us have become like something unclean, and all our righteous acts are like a polluted garment; all of us wither like a leaf, and our iniquities carry us away like the wind."*

It has nothing to do without own righteousness. It has to do with the righteousness of Jesus Christ, which we received when we were saved. Our righteousness comes in us now believing in the completed works of Jesus Christ and what He did on the cross for us.

Satan wants to come to you as the accuser of all the things that you have done and tell you God doesn't love a sinner like you, and that you should give up. But he is a pathological liar!

We have on the breastplate of righteousness when the liar accuses us, the righteousness of Jesus answers it. Don't let the enemy attack your mind with accusations and lies. If you listen to the accuser, he will defeat you. Stand your ground! Remind him of who you are and whose you are. Let the righteousness of Christ deal with him. You put on the breastplate of Jesus. Satan will not be able to respond to this.

3. *"And your feet sandaled with readiness for the gospel of peace"*

A Roman soldier's feet were fitted with sandals called caligae. These sandals were made to help protect the soldiers' feet during long marches into battle. They had extremely thick soles and wrapped perfectly around the ankle of the soldier in a way that protected them against blisters.

Caligae also had spikes at the bottom to help the soldier to stand firm wherever he was. He would stand – he would not be slipping. Believers also have a firm foundation in the gospel. As a believer we are secure in knowing what Jesus has done for us according to **Romans 5:1** *"Therefore, since we have been declared righteous by faith, we have peace with God through our Lord Jesus Christ."*

When we are at peace with God, we can stand, and we can face anything. This is what the Bible says in **Psalm 40:2** *"He brought me up from a desolate pit, out of the muddy clay, and set my feet on a rock, making my steps secure."*

The shoe also gave the Roman soldier mobility. They were able to move around in the heat of the battle. What Paul is saying in "Stand" is that you stand in such a way that you can fight the enemy; that you are able to have mobility. So, when Satan attacks you that you can move, so you can gain territory.

We are content in what we have instead of moving where we ought to be. Look what **Numbers 33: 53** says: *"You are to take possession of the land and settle in it because I have given you the land to possess."* If you don't move forward and possess the land that God has given you, the enemy will possess it.

God promised the children of Israel the land of milk and honey, but on the way to the promised land there were obstacles. God gave them miracle upon miracle. But after that Joshua and his army had to fight for every inch to get to the promised land and they were able to get victory because they were able to stand on the peace of God, knowing that they had peace with God.

Your fight is no different! This peace with God gives us stability and mobility. You will be able to stand firm and nothing will shake you.

4. *"The shield of faith"*

Satan is the greatest doubter. He wants to throw these doubts. Paul compares these doubts as the fiery darts of the wicked.

Have you ever sat and the most ungodly thought come out of nowhere? For no apparent reason? That is what Paul was talking about.

There is no scripture that tells us that Satan can read our minds. But there is a scripture that says he can influence our minds and he wants to throw things at your mind. He is after your mind. When Satan begins to throw these fiery darts, we need to put our faith in God. All the lies, anger, hurt and deception are darts. If Satan can get you to believe a lie, he will get you to live that lie.

How do we put on the shield of God? The Bible says it is simple. By hearing the Word of God.

5. *"The helmet of salvation"*

Satan's main priority is your mind. He will do everything in his power to get hold of your mind. He is after your mind. I cannot stress this enough! He loves to darken and deceive the mind.

So how can we put the helmet of salvation on?

By yielding our minds to the Lord and by saying: "Lord, please give me the mind of Christ, think through me dear Lord and may the mind of Christ be my mind from day to day, thinking God's thoughts and thinking God's principles."

You must intentionally feed your mind with the Word of God. Whether it's reading the Bible, listening to the Bible being read to you or listening to sermons. Whatever works for you. Feed yourself constantly.

You must make an active effort to reprogram your mind into God's mind. That is only possible through God's word. Eventually you find yourself thinking like God, loving what God loves, and hating what God hates. Then having done all this, we take up the sword.

6. *"The sword of the spirit"*

Your correct position in God should be according to **Psalm 89:34**:" *I will not violate my covenant or change what my lips have said."*

Stand on God's promises which surpass human understanding and override the natural world! We stand not under the economy and systems of the world but under the system of God.

For you now stand under two covenants with the Lord. The blood covenant of Jesus Christ (which is your salvation) and the Abrahamic Covenant which says:

2 "I will make you into a great nation, I will bless you, I will make your name great, and you will be a blessing.

3 I will bless those who bless you, I will curse anyone who treats you with contempt, and all the peoples on earth will be blessed through you." – Genesis 12:2–3

God is a rewarder of those who diligently seek him.

Chapter 13
Identifying the Enemy

"Look at Behemoth, which I made along with you. He eats grass like cattle." – Job 40:15

The enemy comes to kill, steal, and destroy!

<u>ENEMY ONE - BEHEMOTH</u>

On 9 September 2021, the Lord gave me a detailed dream about the enemy. I was once again confronted with elephants (as per my dream during the Daniel Fast). I now had to make work of this. This was the second repetition of the sign. By now I knew from scripture that an elephant represented the Behemoth spirit which we find in Job 40:15 – 24. It relates to sin that is invincible, thick-skinned and if not dealt with can no longer remain hidden.

<u>What is Behemoth?</u>
According to the book of Job in Scripture this is a very large powerful grass-eating, river-dwelling creature with bones like bronze pipes and limbs like iron bars. A huge beast that intimidates purely by its size alone.

In the figurative sense this could represent people of high influence in authority, political systems of communism or religious systems of many nations to keep multitudes of people out of the gospel of Jesus Christ.

The Bible states: *"He is the chief of God's works, made to be tyrant over his peers."* The key in this passage is the word tyrant. People, systems, or influences of authority that are Behemoth driven are tyrannical, oppressive, and manipulative. The goal is to dominate.

What is Behemoth known for?

Behemoth is known for its intimidating power, due to its colossal beast like size. It emanates overpowering character with the intent of changing minds or mind-control. To keep those that it has under its spell in the dark of its ways, away from truth. Like the spirit of witchcraft.

People in the dark can't see the woods for the trees.

Suddenly, the saying comes to mind: "There is none so blind as those who do not want to see and none so deaf as those who do not want to hear." Is this starting to make sense? The fact that you can speak the hind leg off a donkey, and it will have no impact whatsoever on an individual who seemingly believes his ways and his faith is the correct way.

Characteristics of Behemoth.

Some of the characteristics of Behemoth are:
- Pride.
- Boastfulness.
- Arrogance.
- Full of self-confidence in their own achievements.
- Resistance of the gospel of truth – resulting in spiritual death.

The Word says in **Proverbs 16:5**: *"Everyone with a proud heart is detestable to the LORD; be assured, he will not go* *unpunished."*

Our confidence is not in our own flesh, but in God and His mighty work through us. True Christianity is based on salvation by grace with our confidence in the shed blood of Jesus Christ.

Where does Behemoth come from?

Scripture tells us in **Job 40:15** – *"Look now at Behemoth, which I made along with you."*

God, the Father created Behemoth together with us when creation was made. Man was created together with all we know. It is man that has opened himself up to demon influence, tyrannical control, and oppression by not residing and abiding in the One, true vine. The Father created us with the ability of choice. In Scripture we read that He gave us the gifts of power, love and a sound mind, so that we may choose wisdom and life in Him.

In **Job 40:19** it is written: *"He (Behemoth) is the first of the ways of God; only He who made him can approach him with His sword."*

Through Him, we were given the ability to speak the word (which is the sword of the Spirit) to defeat the foe. For it is written in Job, that we shall speak and decree a thing and it shall be established. It is but the word of the living God which can defeat all the evil one's works, not only the spirit of Behemoth. This is the only way.

How does God deal with the Behemoths of this world?

Job 34:18-19: *"Is He not the One who says to kings: 'You are worthless and nobles: 'You are wicked', who shows no partiality to princes and does not favor the rich over the poor, for they are all the work of his hands?"*

There is no one that can hide from God. He knows it all as the omnipotent God we serve takes note of all actions everywhere. Not even death can conceal anybody's wicked ways.

Scripture reveals in **Job 34:21-22** *"For His eyes are on the ways of man, and He sees all his steps. There is no darkness nor shadow of death where the workers of iniquity may hide themselves."*

Those that consider themselves better than others in this world, the so-called elite and the seemingly strong and oppressive are the ones that are power hungry. This was a choice they made which brings with it a curse. God uses this sin against them in punishment.

Job explains it so beautifully in detail in **Job 34:23-24** – *"God has no need to examine people further, that they should come before Him for judgment. He breaks in pieces mighty men without inquiry and sets others in their place."*

When God allows the Behemoths in this world to turn against each other, this is usually a public display of destruction.

Job 34:25-26: - *"Therefore He knows their works; He overthrows them in the night, and they are crushed. He strikes them as wicked men in the open sight of others."*

Please take some time and read this account in Job. We serve a living God that never slumbers or sleeps and is never blind to the works of the enemy. But it takes the believer to surrender to Him and abide in His will for our lives, not go astray so we may operate in the power that is deposited in us, that Dunamis, resurrected power to speak against that which is not from God. To make that determined choice to break the bonds and ties in the spirit with the double-edged sword of the Word. What does that mean? One edge of the sword is the written word of God, the other edge is you partnering with God and speaking that word, declaring it into the atmosphere so that it can break in the spirit and off your life!

There is not any creature made by God, that He cannot control. Every ungodly and antichrist system that was put in place by the evil one to stop or deter the message of the good news, will be destroyed by the hand of God. The word tells us that the gates of hell will not prevail against the church. Behemoth will be destroyed.

What does the Behemoth look like in your life?

Sadly, we neglect or don't have the power of discernment when they show up in our lives. Not in the beginning in any event. We are so taken up by their power of presence that it never dawns on us what this influence is.

That presence does not need to do anything but be present. That alone is enough for him to rule. That formidable presence in appearance is enough manifestation to ensure that people sit up and notice, listen and take note of that which comes out of his mouth. He appears strong and intimidates people into passivity. There is no resistance,

Does this sound familiar to you?

Having established this situation, Behemoth rules by showing up or sending his representatives.

This reminds me of the account of a baby elephant being tied to a pole in the ground. It would tug and pull with all its might at first, with no result of freedom. It then gives up the fight because it's come to its own realization that there is no point, as there is no freedom. With time the elephant grows older and as an adult is tied to a mere stake in the ground, but the mind-set and the mind-control has been established. It could easily defy the stake by its strength, but the elephant refuses to try as the limitation in its mind has been firmly established.

Are you seeing the parallel to your situation?

Behemoth systems rule by appearance.

A strategic challenge would be deadly to Behemoth. People in passivity by despair do not attempt an attack. They perceive it as hopeless.

We may think that the evil is unrestrained, but keep in mind that God has got him on His mighty leash. And only by God can he be defeated. The characteristics of Behemoth are also his weaknesses. These can only be challenged and defeated by opposing him with the opposite counter spirit to throw him off balance and expose his vulnerability. For he has no strength outside of God. This Goliath does not need an army to be defeated, it only needs the intervention of our mighty Creator.

Goliath said: "Send one champion against me". Israel waited for that champion. Saul was petrified and promised great riches and popularity. The army was frozen in fear. They needed a David.

The weapon that kills a giant is not the weapon of a warrior. It is the one who stands up against him and is prepared to use the giant's sword against him when the moment of finishing arrives. David could only release the miracle by running into the valley of the giant. It takes partnering with the almighty God and standing with all the might He gives for His purpose. That is our role in life, to come into alignment with His purpose for our life, to partner with Him to defeat the wicked in this world. For the defeat of a system begins with a simple Divine insertion of the opposite spirit! The Spirit of the truth and life.

We need to get to the revelation that the evil is still beneath God's feet and under His reign. May you see Jesus as proof that no innocent suffering is beyond the reach of God's control.

ENEMY TWO – OCTOPUS SPIRIT

On 3 October 2021 I was given a dream where I was using some scissors to cut off an octopus from me. Please refer to **Galations 5: 13 – 25**.

Upon researching this entity, I had revelation upon revelation of truths. To start off with we need to acknowledge and understand the fundamentals of this marine spirit.

What and who is the Octopus Spirit?

Octopus is the Greek word that means "eight feet". The Octopus has six legs and two arms, which is also known as tentacles. These creatures use their size, colours, and flexibility to intimidate and or seduce their victims into their clutches of control. An Octopus is an expert problem solver and can get in and out of almost anything.

They use their weapons to exercise control over their victims through intimidation, domination, and manipulation. Their power lies within their tentacles, ink, strength, speed, agility, and ability to camouflage themselves.

What I have described here is the physical attributes of the bona fide sea creature. But note that the Octopus Spirit operates in the same way. Let's look at their power in literal human-like terms:

- Tentacles: the ability of manipulation to draw their proposed victim in.
- Ink: their words of control and persuasiveness; mind-control and influence.
- Strength: the power of their cunning and deception that

has grown.
- Agility: the speed they come with overpowering love-bombing and the like.
- Ability to camouflage: the quick tongue (in lies) to get them out of numerous tight situations.

Their eight tentacles can represent, but are not limited to:

- Religion
- Fear
- Pride
- Lust
- Greed
- False doctrine
- Deception

The six legs detain their prey, holding it in proximity, by using attacks of oppression upon the prey's physical body and its ability to perform correctly, also by using financial blockage tactics. (Gal 5:7) It deters its prey by holding it back and keeping it from moving forward. (1 Thes 2:8) The two arms draw in the prey by acts of seduction and or bullying and draw their prey into their domain of control and consumption. (Mark 13:22, Rev 2:20)

The ink of the Octopus blinds and confuses, even poison's its victim while it is trying to make it's escape. (1 Thes 2:5; 1 Pet 2:16) The story of Delilah in scripture is a good example of this in operation.

This spirit is also a very strong oppressive spirit that can wrap and intertwine itself into the life of the person (saint or sinner) causing physical deformities, arrested development through mental or brain disorders which is its way of exercising its dominion. (Judges 16:13-19). A good example of this is the self-destruction tendencies of suicide or cutting, oppression and depression, the loss of joy and wanting to live life.

They use their speed and agility to squeeze through the smallest cracks and get themselves out of the most difficult of closed off spaces. They trap their prey in a corner. Watch them operate in lying and deceiving to get out of a situation they have most likely caused. They will manipulate and bully their way into the victim's bank account and bedroom until they get what they want. (Gal 3:1; Jude 1:4) Give these demons a crack and they will find a way to enter and devour! Pornography is a good example of this.

How does this Spirit operate?

We need to be very aware that this species is cunning and revitalizes itself. When one tentacle is cut off it will grow back! This Spirit bends and twists the will and flesh of its victim (prey) until the victim is doing whatever the spirit wants it to do. (2 Tim 2:26).

This spirit is manifested in the life of the victim (a believer) by convincing them to enter ungodly sexual interactions which they represent as a godly union. Their covert operation is in deceiving a person into believing their situation is different. They endeavour to convince others that certain scriptures don't apply to them.

An octopus spirit uses its victim to distort natural desires and fulfill them in deconstructive and distorted ways that are out of alignment with the will of God and what He has ordained for us. This is death! There is a destroying of a person that happens when the sins of the flesh override the ruling of the Spirit. The Spirit becomes weak and the demonic gains dominance. These turn into addictions, obsessive behaviours and destructive patterns and the victim becomes powerless to break free.

This spirit comes in through witchcraft. It is a strongman spirit of mind control that is associated with the squid, mermaid and Leviathan spirits. Ever wonder why you feel that brain fog, anxiousness, and confusion during narcissist abuse?

Conquering the Octopus Spirit.

Cutting off the connections of this spirit (like in my dream) is not enough. However, the dream was a very good comfort that I had gained ground on the spirit but needed to deal with it further. Knowing now that their tentacles grow back, this was not enough.

This took deep confession, repentance of association and wrong choices, and forgiveness. Asking for an everlasting and deep release from God to sever all soul ties and turn one hundred and eighty degrees the other way in changed behaviour. It took everything I got in deep surrender. That is the only way. To combat this spirit, you must armour up with Yahweh's armour, fast and pray.

The impact of this revelation was more than I could think or imagine. But God! Our God is mighty to save.

ENEMY THREE – THE SPIRIT OF JEZEBEL

Who was Jezebel?

Jezebel, was the wicked queen and the wife to the evil King Ahab. She had a reputation for murder, iniquity, and sexual promiscuity. She was the thorn in the side of the prophet Elijah, and also led Israel astray in their foreign worship of idols.(1 Kings 18).

What is the Spirit of Jezebel?

A Jezebel spirit is a demonic influence that creates havoc and strife through cunning, deception, and seduction. Jezebel is driven by sexual appetites, by control and by false teaching. This spirit seeks to dominate and has its own agenda. The spirit operates in man and woman through lust and pornography. It is a controlling spirit through witchcraft and causes fear, flight, and intimidation.

Don't confuse this control with God given authority! This is a controlling spirit that wants you to behave, act or think like them or in a way that best serves them, it is not of God. Holy Spirit gently guides and convicts us. It is Satan who seeks to control, so we can serve his agenda.

Revelation 2:19-25 clearly describes as such:

19 I know your deeds, your love and faith, your service and perseverance, and that you are now doing more than you did at first.

20 Nevertheless, I have this against you: You tolerate that woman Jezebel, who calls herself a prophet. By her teaching she misleads my servants into sexual immorality and the eating of food sacrificed to idols. 21 I have given her time to repent of her immorality, but she is unwilling. 22 So I will cast her on a bed of suffering, and I will make those who commit adultery with her suffer intensely, unless they repent of her ways. 23 I will strike her children dead. Then all the churches will know that I am he who searches hearts and minds, and I will repay each of you according to your deeds.

24 *Now I say to the rest of you in Thyatira, to you who do not hold to her teaching and have not learned Satan's so-called deep secrets, 'I will not impose any other burden on you, 25 except to hold on to what you have until I come.'*

What are the characteristics of the Jezebel Spirit?

- Manipulation - this person is cold and cunning using clever deceptions to manipulate others to get what they want.
- Blasphemy – this individual will do what it can to get the believer to question its faith and beliefs, with the goal of creating doubt and confusion.
- Control – it craves complete control over people and situations and will use what it must to hasten their end game. Also seeking to be the centre of attention and bidding people to do their will.
- Envy- they want what others have, wealth, power, and influence. A sense of entitlement and motivation to obtain these desires.

I share a vivid reminder of a typical event.

Before moving into his home, we were together for a period of almost six years before that second engagement as described earlier in this book. Often, I wear high heel shoes every day of my life. Up to that point before moving into his home, I would most likely wear heels when visiting over the period of years. The moment I relocated, in that first year, I was told to take off my shoes as my heels were making holes in the tiles! After more than six years! And every other woman that entered the house with heels were perfectly excused for not having to remove their shoes. Get your head around that!

Jezebel rules by trying to instill fear, to intimidate or to control. That is not of God. Beware, God does not use fear. Please refer to the scripture I have quoted in 2 Timothy 1:7. This is done by words, guilt, or seduction.

This spirit is found in religious people who claim to follow Jesus, but have no relationship with Him, they are believers but not followers of Christ. This false spirit is deceiving as it shows itself righteous when the opposite is true.

I was given in prayer the words "sugar-coated wickedness" which I refer to in Chapter 14. This made total sense in the context of what I was dealing with.

<u>Jezebel hates the following:</u>
- Authority: they do not like to be controlled
- They hate the word "No". Everything is fine if you do not oppose them.
- They do not like to lose.
- They do not take rebuke or correction.
- There is no repentance or relenting over actions. They do not recognize their wrongdoing.
- They hate the grace of God. They consider it law for you, but grace for them. That is weaponizing and abusing the word of God.
- They hate truthfulness. They are consistently dishonest and sly.

Jezebel didn't want to kill Elijah, she wanted to scare him. She sent a messenger. This spirit brings despair and hopelessness in others. Jezebel pushed Elijah over the edge. Jezebel aims at wearing you out and if that is not enough, seduction and sexual immorality follows. The spirit seduces the servant of God into sexual immorality, through pornography, affairs, and seduction.

Although Jezebel was an idol worshipper. Those individuals we encounter are not Baal worshippers but worship themselves by trying to convince you what good people they are and go so far as to vocalize this themselves. When in truth they are as far removed from God as the pagans.

Remember - a lion has no need to convince you it's a lion!

Jezebel's destruction was due to her resistance to God. Jezebel is strong, but our God is stronger. Jezebel was not repentant. It took a Jehu, that yielded to God to take her down.

Jehu was radical! He meant business and was determined to take Jezebel out. The word says in 2 Kings 9, that Jehu did not go in peace, instead he got in his chariot and charged Jezreel with great speed. Jezebel met him in the last effort of seduction, "by painting her eyes and fixing her hair". She didn't realize that Jehu was anointed and on assignment!

There are consequences by having a Jezebel spirit in your life. Read Rev 2:20-23 again.

The word of God says in 1 **Peter 5:8**

"Be sober-minded, be alert. Your adversary the devil is prowling around like a roaring lion, looking for anyone he can devour."

It was overwhelming to come to a clear understanding of what I was dealing with in the spirit. But in revelation comes liberty and freedom.

Chapter 14
The First Breakthrough

2 "I will go before you and level the uneven places, I will shatter the bronze doors and cut the iron bars in two.
3 I will give you the treasures of darkness and riches from secret places, so that you may know that I am the LORD. I am the God of Israel, who calls you by your name.
4 I call you by your name, for the sake my servant Jacob and Israel my chosen one. I give a name to you though you do not know me.
5 I am the LORD, and there is no other; there is no God but me. I will strengthen you, though you do not know me,
6 so that all may know from the rising of the sun to its setting that there is no one but me. I am the LORD, and there is no other." – Isaiah 45: 2–6

There is no feeling greater than your faith walk seen manifested!

In June 2021, I received a request from a lady on LinkedIn to enter a competition. This competition was a countrywide competition in South Africa calling Personal Assistants to enter for a chance to win the title of South Africa's PA (Personal Assistant) of the Year Award for 2021.

Many years ago, at the beginning of my career, I entered a similar competition and reached the semi-finals in the region. My first instinct was that I could do this. There was a stirring in my spirit that this was the way to go.

There were massive criteria, and the process was quite a lengthy one. But I knew I had to move, I had to go for it, and I had to make this work. I could do the work and the preparation and God will do the rest. I instantly recognized that this was an opportunity to move forward.

One of the criteria was that you had to provide your Facebook, LinkedIn, and Instagram links for them to peruse your life. And like a flood the gratefulness of insight in the previous chapters where I was set apart overwhelmed me. This is why I had to do it. This is why I had to delete and block all social media connections and clean house. Never ignore the unction in your spirit.

When God opens a door for you, you must walk through it!

I immediately had an uphill right out of the starting blocks! The evil one appeared right on par. The first step was that someone nominate you to enter (it could be a fellow PA in the industry). I thought it would be great if my company would do that for me. I was blocked at every turn. I refused to be deterred. Eventually I turned my back and asked a fellow PA to nominate me. We wrote the motivation, and my entry was sent.

Round two started to determine the semi-finalists. This was quite a grueling task and took some serious research and writing. I consulted with various sources and sent the submission.

At this point, I knew I had to work my faith. I decreed my breakthrough, victory in the PA Competition, I prayed Prayers of petition, I sowed seed.

The day arrived and I received an email confirming that I was one of the semi-finalists. Shortly after the email arrived, with new and more criteria to prepare to become one of the finalists.

I had to press on, for whatever was going to move me up and out, was within me and the only thing I knew how to do very well, was my job. I had experience and good experience at that.

I prepared, wrote, and rewrote the submission. I sought wise counsel on my questions and eventually submitted them.

I wrote this Prayer of Petition on 13 August 2021:

Dear Jehovah Jireh,

You, dear Abba Father are the Provider of all! You are the God of more than enough and the Provider of all my needs according to all Your riches and glory.

Abba Lord, today I ask for Restoration in all avenues of my life: –

1. Health (Physical)

I thank you for my healing, Jehovah Rapha. I now request absolute health restoration and guidance in maintaining my health. For Your word says in:

Jeremiah 30:17:

"But I will bring you health and will heal you of your wounds – this is the LORD's declaration – for they call you Outcast, Zion whom no one cares about."

2. Emotional Health and Thinking

I thank you Lord that even this will be well-balanced and of a sound mind Father as according to Scripture it is written in:

2 Timothy 1:7:

"For God has not given us a spirit of fear, but one of power, love and sound judgement."

3. Finance

Abba Father, I pray restoration in my finances Lord, not only for provision Lord, but to prosper and have abundance. In your word it is written Lord in:

Isaiah 61:7

"In place of your shame, you will have a double portion; in place of disgrace, they will rejoice over their share, so they will possess double in their land, and eternal joy will be theirs."

John 10:10

"A thief comes only to steal and kill and destroy. I have come so that they may have life and have it in abundance."

Joel 2: 25–26

25 "I will repay you for the years that the swarming locus ate, the young locust, the destroying locust, and the devouring locust – my great army that I sent against you.

26 You will have plenty to eat and be satisfied. You will praise the name of the LORD your God, who has dealt wondrously with you. My people will never again be put to shame."

Deuteronomy 8:18

"But remember that the LORD your God gives you the power to gain wealth, in order to confirm his covenant he swore to your fathers, as it is today."

Genesis 26:12–14

12 "Isaac sowed seed in that land, and in that year he reaped a hundred times what was sown. The LORD blessed him,

13 and the man became rich and kept getting richer until he was very wealthy.

14 He had flocks of sheep, herds of cattle, and many slaves, and the Philistines were envious of him."

Job 22:21

"Come to terms with God and be at peace; and a flood of water covers you."

4. Family and Relationships

Father, I know that family and unity is important to you. I pray restoration in our family, between my children and with mom. I pray supernatural recovery of all the time that is lost and unity in Jesus' name.

And in this Abba Lord, I include the restoration in marriage with a Godly man of Your choice Father – an evenly yoked bond under Your guidance.

Jeremiah 32:27

"Look, I am the LORD, the God over every creature. Is anything too difficult for me?"

Zachariah 9:12

"Return to a stronghold, you prisoners, who have hope; today I declare that I will restore double to you."

Revelation 21:1–5

1 "Then I saw a new heaven and a new earth; for the first heaven and the first earth had passed away, and the sea was no more.

2 I also saw the holy city, the new Jerusalem, coming down out of heaven from God, prepared like a bride adorned for her husband.

3 then I heard a loud voice from the throne: Look, God's dwelling is with humanity, and he will live with them. They will be his peoples, and God himself will be with them and will be their God.

4 He will wipe away every tear from the eyes. Death will be no more; grief, crying, and pain will be no more, because the previous things have passed away.

5 Then the one seated on the throne said, "Look, I am making everything new" He also said, "Write because these words are faithful and true."

5. <u>Restoration through Victory and Success – PA Competition – Doors to open</u>

Father, I thank you for the keys as shown to me in a dream! I praise you oh Lord for reaching the semi-finals in this competition. To You all the glory God! I couldn't do it without You Father. Now I pray for further guidance and victory towards the final lap of this race.

Nehemia 2:20

"I gave them this reply, "The God of the heavens is the one who will grant us success. We, his servants, will start building, but you have no share, right or historic claim in Jerusalem."

Psalm 37:4

"Take delight in the Lord, and he will give you your heart's desires"

Proverbs 16:3

"Commit your activities to the LORD, and your plans will be established."

Philippians 4:13

"I am able to do all things through him who strengthens me."

6. <u>Restoration through Victory over Enemies, Oppression and Injustice</u>

Lord, I lift up my current home situation with him to You again dear Father. I lay it by Your feet and ask You to deal with the injustice – due to broken promises. Vengeance is not mine Lord – therefore I pray that You make a way in this wilderness and a river through this desert oh God!

For it is written:

Isaiah 45:2

"I will go before you and level the uneven places; I will shatter the bronze doors and cut the iron bars in two."

Psalm 37: 28–29

28 "For the LORD loves justice and will not abandon his faithful ones. They are kept safe forever, but the children of the wicked will be destroyed.

29 The righteous will inherit the land and dwell in it permanently."

Ecclesiastes 2:26

"For to the person who is pleasing in his sight, he gives wisdom, knowledge and joy; but to the sinner he gives the task of gathering and accumulating in order to give to the one who is pleasing in God's sight. This too is futile and a pursuit of the wind."

Thank you El Shaddai – to You all the Glory and the Honor! Amen.

Shortly after this in my quiet time, I requested from the Lord in prayer how to deal with the situation at home at this point. The silence in prayer brought me two words: *sugar-coated wickedness*.

I was stunned! I pressed in and continued to ask that the Father part the Red Sea for me that I may exit the door on dry land. For the word was explicit that the Lord is no respecter of persons, what he did for one, he would do for another. As he did for Moses, I had full trust that he would do for me.

The next email arrived. I was in the top finals! I made it to the final six in the competition! In the top six of one hundred and fifty entries in the country. I literally sank down on my knees in overwhelming gratefulness. The wheel was turning.

Now only a final online interview would determine the winner. A week's preparation of thinking and rethinking all kinds of possible questions. The day arrived and the interview was wrapped up.

Following this, arrangements were made to fly to Johannesburg and spend the night at the hotel in preparation for the great event that would be broadcast live on YouTube, and the winner announced.

We were three finalists from Cape Town and three from Johannesburg. My fellow peers all had their flight tickets purchased by their employers, I however had to cover my own. In addition to this I had to find my own way to the airport in Cape Town and put in an unpaid day's leave. I did what I needed to do and went.

By now, I had made friends with one of the competitors who also was from Cape Town. We arranged to share the same flight, met at the airport, and got down to getting to know each other.

We became friends and found that we had a lot in common, exchanged stories of our profession and had a good laugh at some.

The day arrived and the nerves were somewhat high. I had to rest in the faith, that I did what I could, and it was now up to God.

My fellow colleague that travelled with me, was awarded the win and the title.

At the lunch afterwards, we were told that the scores were exceptionally close and that there was literally a half point difference between some. I was not deterred. The experience and having this wonderful interaction with PA's from other walks and spheres of life made me realize that I needed to step up my game. I needed to move, and I needed to move quickly and upward. I had to start taking stock of where I was and what I needed to do to up the game.

This exposure to my career was only half of the great chance that was ahead of me. As one of the six finalists we were now obliged to contribute our time and resources into a project that would give back into the industry. The topic was under a huge spotlight, and we were each partnered, with an individual overseas who specialized in the field. I was ecstatic at the thought of this. This project was concentrated on research, preparation of questions and a live online interview with your international partner that would be recorded. All these interviews would be combined into a video that would be uploaded to YouTube as a contribution to the future of the industry.

I started to understand the concept that your talent will make room for you.

Proverbs 22:29

"Do you see a person skilled in his work? He will stand in the presence of kings. He will not stand in the presence of the unknown."

Chapter 15
Worship Is Your Weapon

25 "About midnight Paul and Silas were praying and singing hymns to God, and the prisoners were listening to them. 26 Suddenly there was such a violent earthquake that the foundations of the jail were shaken, and immediately all the doors were opened, and everyone's chains came loose." – Acts 16:25–26

Worship changes us!

When on an airline and in the event of an emergency due to a drop in air pressure, the oxygen masks drop. You are encouraged to put your mask on first and then assist other passengers.

Immediately the saying of "Charity starts at home" comes to mind! It starts with you first.

Jesus came to us and came to rescue us first. How does that affect you personally?

Think about this for a moment. God owns our body, our spirit, our life, and our possessions. The only thing that we can give God that he did not give us – is worship!

Sometimes we like the idea of worship as singing our favorite songs, more than the surrender through worship. Worship is about your surrender, your pursuit of His presence.

In **Genesis 22:5**, we find the first words regarding worship: "Then Abraham said to his young men, *"Stay here with the* *donkey, the boy and I will go over there to worship; then we'll come back to you."* There were no singers or songs involved. This was about an altar and a knife. This expresses the health of your obedience to God.

The word says: *"But an hour is coming, and is now here, when the true worshippers will worship the Father in Spirit and in truth."* – **John 4:23**

What matters is your heart. Personal transformation does not happen without worship. Worship does not happen without surrender. Worship does not happen without obedience.

Once there is genuine worship there will always be a counterfeit. Fake worshippers are the confirmation that there are true followers of Jesus. Don't be distracted if someone is faking it. Herod did not want to go to worship, he sent someone else to do it for him. No one can worship on your behalf!

Our tongues do not break bones, but it can break people. We hurt people and are hurt by people with our words. God doesn't want us to worship and yet lie, mistreat, and deceive people and live a nightmare at home. Herod said he would worship and turned around and killed babies!

Counterfeit worship is the worship that is all fair and well until the proverbial you-know-what hits the fan! They are the seed in the ground that when the sun comes up, they scorch and die. Their faith is only alive until a problem appears. Be careful if something does not go your way to then start blaming God.

I did not win the PA competition, but I used the door to change my life to climb higher and do more than what the win could bring me. It was the catalyst!

Please see and acknowledge this.

God is not something you use. He is the God you worship. He is the Master of the universe.

Reality is that sometimes it is difficult to reconcile God's goodness to what is happening in our lives. Understand that God doesn't exist for you. You exist for Him.

He never promised in His Word that everything will go our way. He promised that His Son will be the way, even if I don't get my way. As long as I am on His way everything will be all right. He will surprise you beyond your wildest dreams!

God cannot personally fix us if we don't genuinely worship Him. When you worship for real God takes your problems and brings progress to your life. He begins to change your life.

God will give you blessings instead of worry.

God will give you peace instead of paranoia.

God will give you confidence instead of insecurity.

When you come before Him burdened, God will come in and give you the joy and peace. God will turn your wounds into scars and your scars into stars!

When you come before God and lie prostrate before him, your life will never be the same.

God wants you to sing in the storm. Look what happened to Paul and Silas in jail when they worshipped at midnight. You must be healthy on the inside. You cannot be healthy if you don't worship.

Worship is bending our will. Our problem with character is that our will is too stiff. We are stuck up and stubborn. The older we are the harder it is to bend. If you don't bend your will in worship, life will break your will in crisis! Life will crush your will.

When you bend your will and say: "Lord not my will, but Your will be done," and truly worship your will becomes flexible. You become pliable in the hand of God and in your circumstances. You bend like a palm tree that yields in the storm, and when the storms pass you come right back up.

The Word says, that when the storm hit Job's life, he fell down and worshipped.

God wants to take control of your life. You need to surrender and lie prostrate before Him if you want to see change.

I encourage you to sing.

Sing and worship in spirit and in truth!

At the top of your voice.

Sing, child of God, Sing!

Chapter 16
Your Talent Will Make Room for You

10 "Just as each one has received a gift, use it to serve others, as good stewards of the varied grace of God.
11 If anyone speaks, let it be as one who speaks God's words; if anyone serves, let it be from the strength God provides, so that God may be glorified through Jesus Christ in everything. To him be the glory and the power forever and ever." – 1 Peter 4: 10–11

Success is not dependent on talent alone; you have to work your talent!

A week after returning to Cape Town with the personal victory, I drove to work one morning, still saying my decrees and singing worship. I knew that the time had come that I had to work on repackaging myself and find out what I require to move me up that desired step I so desperately required. I cannot tell you where the thought came from, but I in my spirit knew I had to find myself a career coach.

I spent time on the internet and randomly found an individual whom I thought would fit the bill of what I required. This I also realise, was not random, but a divine intervention. The man whom I contacted was highly reputable and worked with various large companies to restructure and assist the profiles of their individuals. I was in good company.

I explained my position, how I saw the move forward and

what I thought was required. We immediately hit it off. He knew exactly what the problem was, and we undertook to work together for at least two months to get down to basics and analyze my position in the market.

This was done in tandem with my research with my international partner in the PA project.

I fully submerged myself into research and study for the following three months. It took interviews with fellow PA's, consulting with SA's PA of the Year for 2018, digging deep into finding what new technology I wasn't up to scratch with, doing online courses and digging up information on current ways and courses for new PAs in the market.

I closed my eyes to the outside world and forcefully blazed my trail through it all! I knew this was leading to the door I wanted to have opened – the door for a new high echelon position I was seeking.

Mid-September the Day of Atonement arrived. The Day of Atonement is Yom Kippur, a Jewish holiday devoted to atoning for sins. It's considered the holiest day of the year in Judaism. Observation of the day is marked by fasting and prayers of repentance.

This would set the tone for the ensuing year for your life. This is also mentioned in our Bible for the followers of Jesus and a practice that I had adopted.

The full description can be found in **Leviticus 16**. I now refer specifically to verses 30–31:

30 "Atonement will be made for you on this day to cleanse you, and you will be clean from all your sins before the LORD.

31 It is a Sabbath of complete rest for you, and you must practice self-denial; it is a permanent statute."

I adhere to this annually and make Jesus my business, order

my life and set the tone for the ensuing year. Although we as followers of Christ adhere to a Gregorian calendar, the Hebrew calendar of God is very much alive in the Word.

During my research, I was advised by the PA of the Year for 2018 during our interview, that I consider doing a live video interview with myself. Sharon had become a good friend in the interim and we discussed the methods of marketing me with optimum effect and impact. I immediately understood the methodology and why this would be effective, post COVID. We discussed an incident where this proved to be very successful during an application process.

I discussed this with my son, who had a friend that did this kind of recording and could edit the content and see to the technological aspect for me at no charge!

Once again, I started preparing the questions, liaised the answers with Sharon, the language and vocabulary with another friend and set out to memorize and rehearse all I could during the December holidays of 2021.

I was determined to submit this on my return to work at the commencement of business in the new year of 2022. I earmarked the companies I would like to work at and amended my one-page CV to give it a totally fresh look. Together these would be submitted to where I would like to be placed.

You have heard the saying before that old ways don't open new doors. I was convinced in my spirit that if I wanted to go where I had the deep nestled desire to go, it was imperative that I do what most others didn't do. That I would set a benchmark that would differentiate me from others in the workforce.

At the beginning of January 2022, I entered my second Daniel Fast for twenty-one days to set the tone for the year. With clear objectives for a new job and a new home, and the grace to keep my sanity in the current situation! Upon receiving my first salary at the end of January I sowed my first fruit seed. I will address the importance of this in a next chapter.

At the end of January, the edited version of the recorded interview was complete, my CV amended, and I was ready to start launching into new territory.

My project with my international partner, Peggy Vasquez from Washington State in the US, was recorded and I could now devote my time to seek alternate employment fully and boldly. My profile was changed on LinkedIn and my whole image brought into alignment and upgraded to where I wanted to go.

Within a month after I started submitting my CV and interview video, I was contacted by a recruitment agent who saw my particulars. She was thrilled and excited and requested a Skype interview on a Saturday afternoon!

I continued to pray and decree.

After the initial interview with the requesting company, a second interview was called. Walking out of this, I hardly reached my car and a message arrived on my phone to ask for figures for negotiation. I knew this was it!

At the end of April, I resigned, and I had to work a two months' notice period as per my employment contract. Do you remember the dream in the beginning chapters of the wooden desk and the job explanation? Do you now understand the significance of a dream journal?

We are made by Christ Jesus into good works, and he has predestined us to walk a certain path. Each one's path is unique to his/her own talents and gifts. God has ordained us to works and opportunities that will come forth to do things. He will provide the provision for you to accomplish this.

Your difference is in your design!

Ask the Lord: "What are my strengths and gifts and what are my weaknesses? Show me areas that I need to work on, so I can please You." A lesson I learnt from Dr. Jolynne Whittaker.

Jeremiah 1:5

"I chose you before I formed you in the womb; I set you apart before you were born. I appointed you a prophet to the nations."

People around you will see your work. The execution of your gifts is unique as well. You won't do things the way others do them.

Ephesians 2:10

"For we are his workmanship, created in Christ Jesus for good works, which God prepared ahead of time for us to do."

Your gift makes room for you. Things will begin to shift for you.

The power of operating in your gift ensures success.

Chapter 17
Seed Time and Harvest Time

2 "The LORD answered me: Write down the vision; clearly inscribe it on tablets so one may easily read it.
3 For the vision is yet for the appointed time; it testifies about the end and will not lie. Though it delays, wait for it, since it will certainly come and not be late." – Habbakuk 2:2–3

SOW FOR A HARVEST!

Whatever is seen in the natural was formed in the spirit first. Kingdom principles are echoed in natural manifestations. The Lord's instructions are very clear in that we need to sow to produce a harvest. Harvest does not fall out of thin air. The word says that faith without works is dead.

God will meet your faith and do what you cannot do, but you need to work with what you have up to the point where your efforts cannot take you further.

I completely got to grips with the principle of sowing and reaping with my words. I share here the mechanics of the sowing and reaping with your seed to ensure your harvest.

Habbakuk tells us to write the plan and make it clear. This is what the Prayer of Petition is that I have covered in various chapters. Vague prayers bring vague results. Stand on specific scripture to back-up your prayers.

1. <u>Determine your harvest</u>

What is it that you want to see? Be specific.

When a matter is deeply engraved on your heart, do business with it. Don't wait for the perfect time. There is a window to get seed in the ground and to reap, according to **Ecclesiastes 11:4** – *"One who watches the wind will not sow, and the one who looks at the clouds will not reap."*

2. <u>Check your heart posture</u>

What do I mean by that?

According to scripture when we pray, our hearts will always be bowed in adoration, gratitude, and humility to our loving God, for we know that His eyes are open and ears attentive to the prayers of His people. The most important part of sowing is the heart behind the gift. So, when you sow, be sure you are acting as a good sower. When you give in sorrow, there is no faith, so there is no return. Sow your seed in joy and you will reap a harvest.

3. <u>Ask the Lord how much to sow</u>

He will guide you.

It is important that we have money, but that money doesn't have us. Understand that seed produces after its own kind according to Proverbs 16:9.

When you sow food into a church or organization, be ensured that you too will be blessed with food somewhere along the line. I have tested this. I blessed someone with several pairs of shoes, and sure enough a week later I received shoes! Seed is anything you give. It can be time, money, resources, faith, hope or love.

When we sow financial seed, we will receive a financial

harvest.

Jesus said in **Luke 6:38** *"Give, and it will be given to you; a good measure – pressed down, shaken together, and running over – will be poured into your lap. For with the measure you use, it will be measured back to you."*

That's a powerful truth! That's why the enemy doesn't want you to participate in sowing.

4. <u>Ask the Lord for the seed and the ground</u>

There are times when we truly don't have the financial seed to sow for our Prayers of Petition or the purpose for which we intend it. The word tells us in **2 Corinthians 9:10** – *"Now the one who provides seed for the sower and bread for food will also provide and multiply your seed and increase the harvest of your righteousness."*

This is the time to pray to God to provide you with the seed to sow as the word clearly states that He will provide seed for the sower. It will surely appear!

Determine from God, in which ground you need to sow. He will guide you and you will have an unction in your spirit, whether it was a message that you listened to or the ministry that you are fed. Understand that seed needs to be sowed into good ground where a harvest is ensured. Ground that works with your seed to produce a sound harvest, ground where it is evident that seed grows!

5. <u>Name your seed</u>

I keep a journal of the seeds that I have sown, where I have sown them to, the amount and the date. This helps me keep track of my seed. When you name your seed, believe that your words have power! According to Mark 11:23–24.

Keep track of your seed by means of your journal and water your seed with prayer according to 2 Corinthians 1:20. Pray now with praise and thanksgiving and speak God's word over your seed. You can also water your seed with additional seed as you are led by Holy Spirit.

6. *Call in the harvest!*

You must not only be a good giver or sower, but you also need to be a good reaper too!

Your harvest is determined by what you do while you're waiting for it. Waiting is the toughest part of the sowing process. A lot is dependent upon how you wait.

If you sow your seed in faith, you will expect it to grow, and you will keep expecting – no matter how long it takes. In the meantime, it is important that your words match your faith. You need to start *declaring* that you are expecting a record-breaking harvest!

Mark 4: 29:

"*As soon as the crop is ready, he sends for the sickle, because the harvest has come.*"

What is the sickle? The sickle is a blade, the two-edged sword of the word of God! Speak! Lift your voice, declare, and call it in from the South, the East, the North and the West.

God remembers every seed you've ever sown. Don't give up on your seed just before the finish line. Harvest is coming!

7. *Weed your crop*

The reality is the enemy is also at work and you need to keep the weeds out of your crop.

What can choke your crop?

Unforgiveness, bitterness and strife.

Keep a watch on your heart, pull the "weeds" out by the roots when they crop up, spray them with the Word and cast them out with the help of the Holy Spirit. I had to do this *daily* for a very, very long time. I address this in the chapter of Binding and Loosing

8. *First Fruit Seed*

I mentioned the First Fruit Seed in the previous chapter that I sowed after the Daniel Fast in the beginning of the year, with that first salary.

Without going into an in-depth explanation, I would like to show you the importance of honoring God with your first and best.

Exodus 23:19

"Bring the best of the first fruits of your land to the house of the LORD your God. "

Committing yourself to the Lord in the beginning of the year through fasting (with clear objectives for that year) and then honoring the Father at the end of the fast with your first fruits offering, shows obedience to the Lord. You honor God when you bring Him the first fruits of your increase. By offering the first fruits of the increase of your substance, you demonstrate that God is number one in your life. When you make God your priority, He will make you, His priority.

The first fruit represents our first increase on any new venture that we embark on. The first fruit offering brings in the hundred-fold blessing. These are appointments that He has made to reconnect us to Him and the blessing, not to get something from us, but to get something to us.

Interestingly, first fruit in Hebrew is the word "bikkurim" and literally means "promise to come." And God is not a man that He should lie, His promises never return void.

Chapter 18
Binding and Loosening

"I will give you the keys of the kingdom of heaven, and whatever you bind on earth will have been bound in heaven, and whatever you loose on earth will have been loosed in heaven." – Matthew 16:19

Heaven is allowing what we allow!

We have been given the authority to rule and reign with Jesus on the earth. We have also been "given the authority to trample on snakes and scorpions, and no harm shall come nigh us."

1 Timothy 6:12 says: *"Fight the good fight of faith. Take hold of eternal life to which you were called and about which you have made a good confession in the presence of many witnesses."*

It is not all up to God what we do here on earth. God loved us so much that He gave us the ability of choice. He did, however, give us the keys to the Kingdom of Heaven to assist us in our daily walk and fight against the wiles of the enemy.

By now, you are fully aware that the enemy's biggest attack is through deception and lies. I speak about this throughout this book. The result of deception and lies is that these get exposed at some point and the result is disillusionment, anger, hatred, and bitterness. This is the enemy's ultimate trap. If we do not deal with these elements in our lives this pulls us deeper into the pit of sin, blocking blessings, favor, and breakthrough.

When, in the midst of absolute turmoil this can be a very tall order! Especially when you have thoughts of swinging a baseball bat to re-arrange someone's face to an unrecognizable pulp! And to top it all think you will absolutely rock that orange overall!

I must be honest. There were days where I asked God if He had some spare time. I would swing the bat if He would like to do some healing afterwards! I had to repent.

There was an abnormal amount of deep nestled anger within me towards him, the situation, and the injustice against me. This manifested in all sorts of ways, from tears, outbursts to hatred.

In my daily search on YouTube for a message, I stumbled (and no I don't believe in coincidence) on the teachings of Kat Kerr. I humbly share these here with you. This was a game changer for me.

You say out loud in the name of Jesus:

I loose from my soul all unforgiveness, bitterness and hatred towards him (name the person's name).

I loose from my soul all ill thoughts regarding him and his family.

I loose from my soul all words that have been spoken to me, over me and against me.

I loose from my soul all fear regarding this situation.

I loose from my soul all emotions tied to him.

I loose from my soul all soul ties with him.

I loose from my soul all unforgiveness towards myself for this situation.

The hand of God literally sets you free from all of this and removes it from your soul and your life. I had to do this several times as regards to unforgiveness, bitterness and hatred whenever my emotions crept up on me. Forgiveness is a daily crucifying of the flesh.

You follow the loosing from your soul by binding the following to your soul in replacement:

I bind to my soul the love of God.

I bind to my soul the absolute forgiveness of God.

I bind to my soul the peace and rest of God.

I bind to my soul the hope and faith in God.

I bind to my soul healthy respect and self-love, like God loves me.

I bind to my soul the wisdom given by God.

I bind to my soul the thoughts of God.

It is necessary to replace the cleared space in your soul with that which you require.

I had only practiced binding and losing in terms of binding the enemy into submission for example, in failing in his attempts in my life. Obviously, in more detail as to a specific situation. Never had I given thought that losing something would set you free, out from it, which is the counteractive use of this principle.

Revelations kept coming on this journey.

I encourage you to make time, come to some rest and acknowledge that within you there might be issues holding you back. Write some notes and set yourself free by actively getting rid of it all.

This is a good first step.

Chapter 19
Working Your Plan and Planning Your Work

"A person's heart plans his way, but the LORD determines his steps." – Proverbs 16:9

Submitting my exit plan to God – the joy immeasurable!

The day, I returned from the PA Competition in Johannesburg on the plane, was the day I decided to start doing the math for what I required to move. I didn't know how at that time, but I knew I could start getting back to basics and make lists.

The list was long and costly, and I had to start cleaving at it month-by-month to do what I could. I trusted God to come through for me as there was no way that I could cope with this massive financial expense in one shot. It was insurmountable.

I did what I knew how. I prayed, wrote the Prayer of Petition again, fasted and sowed. Shortly after that, God gave me a vision – as clear as a Netflix movie shot! He showed me His hand, holding all my seed that I had sown! This was enough for me to know He heard me, my seed was in His hand, and I can move forward to do what I could.

Every month I would purchase what I could on my list and store my goods at the house of a friend. I'd seek the best prices of goods online and have them delivered to the office. On my way home, I'd drop them off at the friend's house. Over time I covered the basics but had a few large and costly items that I still needed to purchase. I still didn't know how.

The day I signed the contract for my new job, I realized that I had a provident fund at my current employer, which I had access to and suddenly the lights came on! I sped off to my broker and discussed the implications of my withdrawal, the tax, and the best way of applying these funds towards my new proposed life. In addition, I have the most wonderful mother who assisted me. Words and thank you's could never express my immense gratitude.

Have you any idea the joy that bubbled up inside of me?

I started making plans, seeking a new home, and redoing the math and the budget.

I made a determined effort to seek God deeper, wanting to have absolute clear guidance in His ways. I would drive to work early in the morning, firstly to avoid the heavy traffic, but secondly to spend the time before work in my car with the Lord. This was His time. I knew that after my praise and worship in singing, God inhabits my praises, and this was the time that I could hear Him very clearly.

He instructed me to keep a journal and pen handy and that when He speaks, I should write. I couldn't understand this at first, I was uncertain that I would hear with my eyes open to write when I concentrated so hard with my eyes closed to hear His voice.

I share here the message I was given on 27 May 2022:
My child,
Your voice reaches far in the spirit world.
The angels rejoice with you.

Child of mine,
Your joy is heartfelt – I like that,
We're going places, child.

Liesel, I know you have a lot on your plate,
But together we will get through it.
Keep your focus and the end result in mind.

I'm pouring into you what you asked for this morning.
Your victory is sure.

My child, my hand is resting on your soul.
Do not be perturbed.
Yes, my peace is in you in this last stretch.
It's the home stretch, my child.

Liesel, lift your mind and your thoughts higher.
Come settle with me.
Here is lots to see.
I will show you.

I want you to experience my glory in greater ways.
You will then see what I see.
Yes, you are seated in heavenly places with me.
But I want your focus to rise higher, child.
More of me and less of the world.
I want to give you spiritual eyes and ears that you have asked for.
It is coming, child, for my work and way.
I want you to see the host,

And see the results of your words that you speak.
My child, you are having impact in the spiritual world,
And it is manifesting in the natural.

You are hearing my word,
And it too is being confirmed by my prophets.
Soon, you will also stand in that position,
For the mantle is yours.
Yours to speak my word as I say it.

In you, I am planting more excitement.
Your cup will overflow.
It is coming forth.
My work is destined for glory through you.
Are you excited, child?
(Yes! Father)

Me too! Child,
And we will spend lots of time together.
Talking, planning, and writing.
Be prepared.
You will do it all for me,
And it will flow, child – don't worry.
It is I that will write.

Your home is my home – I like that.
Thank you for that dedication, child.
I will show up and we will sit together.
You have made a way for me to enter,
I will come.

Child, get in the habit of keeping pen and paper at your

bedside.
For I come and I speak at my will.
You made the space, child,
I will be there.

Lieseltjie, listen to me,
I am holding you tight.
You won't fall.
Keep going, child.
I won't leave you nor forsake you.

The ride and road might be bumpy,
But you are under my wing,
And walk in my favor and glory.

Yes, child, the Tsunamis might come,
But you will stand like the fruit tree,
Anchored in me.
You will not be uplifted.

Stand, child, Stand!

Don't fear words.
I cancel them in the spirit.
Attacks will be changed into blessings for you.
Walk in confidence, child.
For it is I walking and you in me.
I love your way, child – for it is mine.
Speak my word for all to hear.
I want you to know that this new life is very different.
Not what you are used to and know.
This life in me is fun,

But it is fun in me not of the world.
You have learnt to walk in the Spirit,
And my world of heaven excites you.
It will now become your reality and destination.
A place to visit and refresh.
You have asked.

My child, I've got your heart,
And it beats for me.
I will show you what is coming.

I've got every prayer in my hand.
And yours I hold close.
Yes, child, you have my ear.
Child, walk tall this day,
I've got your back.

Give me a hug, child.
Teach my children how to hug me.

You think I wasn't undone?
Tears were streaming down my face.

Chapter 20
The Red Sea vs The Jordan

21 "Then Moses stretched out his hand over the sea. The LORD drove the sea back with a powerful east wind all that night and turned the sea into dry land. So the waters were divided, 22 and the Israelites went through the sea on dry ground, with the waters like a wall to them on their right and their left." – Exodus 14:21–22

Deliverance vs The Promised Land!

We all know the story in the Bible of the exodus of the Israelites from Egypt and their journey in the desert for forty years and due to disobedience never entered the promised land. The most iconic part where Moses came to the Red Sea and the Lord parted the seas so they could walk through on dry land to freedom.

In my quiet time with the Lord over a lengthy period, I knew and understood that in my prayers I had to pray scripture to God, to remind him of his promises. He says in His Word to keep him in remembrance of His promises. I cannot even begin to think the number of times that this was my prayer:

Dearest Abba Father, Jesus and Holy Spirit,
I praise and worship You for who You are. I thank you for

being my Abba Father and that You know me by name.

Lord, Your ways are higher than my ways, Your thoughts are higher than mine. You oh God level the mountains and make the crooked places straight.

You, Father break the gates of bronze and bend the bars of steel. You bring water from the rock, make ways in the wilderness and rivers in the desert.

I pray in the mighty name of Jesus that You will please part the Red Sea for me that I may exit this front door on dry land for good. Lord, I know that You are no respecter of persons and what You did for Moses You are willing and well able to do for me.

Thank you, Father, that I can live in expectation of your goodness.

Amen

Little did I know that this was the prayer of deliverance! I could see the signs of freedom, but only recently realized that freedom is deliverance! It took obedience and living holy to obtain deliverance.

After signing my new employment contract, I knew deliverance was there. I was unstoppable.

I made plans like a woman possessed. The promised land was in sight. But it wasn't just for the taking.

It took work, negotiation, planning, pressing on and planning more. Remember Joshua?

Joshua 3:2–4

2 "After three days the officers went through camp,

3 and commanded the people: "When you see the ark of the covenant of the LORD your God carried by the Levitical priests, you are to break camp and follow it.

4 But keep a distance of about a thousand yards between

yourselves and the ark, don't go near it, so that you can see the way to go, for you haven't travelled this way before."

When you come through deliverance, and the season has shifted to walk into your promised land there is protocol, preparation, and surrender. This is new level faith.

I distinctly remember another vision the Father gave me in this time. The clear picture of a kitchen. The place of preparation.

Preparation in God's way and on His timeline.

When the door to your promised land opens and you cross the proverbial Jordan in obedience and the guidance of God, the disgrace of Egypt will be rolled away from you (Joshua 5:9).

Understand also, that as with Gideon (in Judges 7) the Lord reduced his troops from twenty thousand to ten thousand to ultimately three hundred men. Only those who drank from the river with their hands to their mouths looking forwards were chosen. The rest who lapped the water with their tongues were disqualified.

Your promised land is for you, not for all around you. A select few who can look forward with you will join your walk. It is natural in this time that people fall away and don't understand your journey. They make space for the new to come in. That is God's way.

Revelation 21:5

"Then the one seated on the throne said, "Look, I am making everything new." He also said, "Write, because these words are faithful and true."

Chapter 21
Time with God

"Because the LORD is jealous for his reputation, you are never to bow down to another god. He is a jealous God." – Exodus 34:14

Building a relationship with the Father.

Idols – let's look at this for a moment. The Bible tells us that idolatry is the worship of someone or something other than God as though it were God. Putting something or everything else above God.

How many things in our daily existence don't we spend more time with and pay attention to, than God? We already need to do our daily jobs which takes a chunk of our time and dedication – just to get home and be hooked on television, Facebook, Instagram, YouTube, cellphones and who knows what else that consumes our minds. Then we still have family and children and the rest of the balls we keep in the air!

And more often, than not the proverbial monkeys fly and hit the walls and we burn and crash – why me God? Where is God?

Busy-ness is the enemy of spirituality.

Matthew 6:33

"But seek first the kingdom of God and his righteousness, and all these things will be provided for."

God wants to be first in your life. He deserves to be first in your life. He is your Creator! We need to treat Him and acknowledge Him as such in our daily lives. Yet sadly we more than often don't.

When we meet someone new in our life, this is an all-consuming feeling of wanting to spend time with that person, showering that person with love and vice versa. Or so it is supposed to be. We make every possible effort to build that relationship to flourish and walk in it to a desired end of union.

So why is it different when it comes to God?

The Bible tells us that He loved the world so much that He sent his only begotten Son to die for us so we may have eternal life. The ultimate and most sacrificial act any Father could ever do! And it was for you – and for me! So, we can spend time eternal with Him in the most glorious place called heaven.

That we may be part of His home, thoughts, life, ways, and magnificence. This is what the word says of God in:

James 1:17

"Every good and perfect gift is from above, coming down from the Father of lights, who does not change like shifting shadows."

He is the ultimate light of absolute goodness! His focus is you and me for a hope and a future with an expected end. Grab hold of this.

Towards the end of my time in the "madhouse," I was blessed with being on my own quite often when he would go out to wherever he went. I started to get the picture of building a relationship with God. I used this time to actively work on spending time with Abba Father.

I would pray in the morning and make an appointment with

Him for afternoon tea. I would go about my chores during the day and stop by the shop and buy cake for the event. I couldn't wait until the time would arrive and the house was empty, and I could have the solace of calm and quiet – even if only for a few hours!

I would boil the kettle, set out the plates and make tea and plate the cake for two.

Did you know that Jesus liked sweet things? The word tells us that He enjoyed honey and honeycomb. He has a sweet tooth! There is nothing on this earth that is not in Heaven. For it is written "that it be on earth as it is in heaven"! Not only did He bring water from the rock, but he brought forth honey from the rock for Moses in Deuteronomy 32:13. Jesus knows about the good stuff.

On the couch, I would settle down and make myself comfortable as if having time with a friend I love very dearly. I'd offer Him His plate and put it aside and start the conversation, have a bit of my slice of cake and a sip of tea and speak my mind. During this time, I also learnt to be quiet. I wanted to hear the voice of Jesus. Sitting in silence until the knowingness in my spirit filled me.

I told God how much I loved Him, that I am so grateful that He chose me and that I am His precious daughter. That He showed me through the love of His eyes how He looks at me, as beautiful, gracious, and worth living.

My thank yous were deep and heartfelt for the road ahead, the wonderful expectation I could live in and that I want to have a relationship with Him. I asked if we could deepen this relationship. Could we please have more meaningful time together? Can I too write what I believe He is telling me.

In this time, I would make a second cup of tea.

I spoke about experiencing a tangible reality of God in my

life. At times, I would clasp my hands together and tighten the grip as if squeezing.

Spirit made me understand: "Thank you for the hug." Scripture says: "God in you, the hope of glory." I understood that He is in me – and me pressing my hands together, in the act of worship or prayer is him in me together with my physical body coming together in a hug so to speak.

Since then, I have been hugging God every single day and blowing Him kisses at every encounter. He is **my** Abba Father, the Restorer of **my** soul!

He is real.

He is in me.

He is with me and never ever leaves me.

I have told you that every morning before work, I would dedicate the time to Him. This was His time to speak after my praise and worship and He chose the topic. I share here a snippet of one.

I am not at liberty to share all these encounters as they are sacred, and I have not been given the authority by God to do so but share extracts where appropriate in this book.

On 28 May 2022:

My child, come and just rest in me.

Let me show you what that means.

Your strength I am building – more resilience.

Child of mine,

You are in my hand,

I am holding you with open freedom,

Freedom in me.

Freedom in glory.

Hope and a future.

Sing a song of joy my child,

For the new is at hand.
The new all will see.
The new I am bringing to thee.

Dance for me, my child,
Celebration is at hand,
On earth as it is in heaven.
The victory sound has come – rejoice!

Your song will bring victory to others,
And rejoicing will follow.
Hope will be attainable for all.
My promises stand firm and sure.
Teach them to stand on my promises,
Speak them,
Declare them,
Pray them,
And believe them.
Stand in faith!
That they will come to pass.
Rejoicing will then surely come.
Tell them, child!
You know how it works.

I encourage you to become more God aware, this is a relationship that goes beyond your wildest dreams. Make time for your Father, put Him first. It opens the understanding of the Word and deepens your prayer life.

Pick a flower, say thank you and put it in a vase for Him! He sees you and wants to share your day.

Hug Him and tell Him you love him! For He loves you more than you can ever imagine.

Chapter 22
Goodbyes…

"Write to the angel of the church in Philadelphia: Thus says the Holy One, the true one, the one who has the key of David, who opens and no one will close, and who closes and no one opens." – Revelation 3:7

When God opens the way, it opens. When God closes the door, it closes.

By now, I had worked the first month of my resignation period of two months. Also, the time had come where the necessary conversation of my departure from the "madhouse" was to take place. I worked on the plan and laid it before God and made my arrangements that I would leave my current employer on 24 June 2022.

All the relocation arrangements were set in place, booked, and paid for. I had plenty of logistical things to still take care of, but the base of all was set in motion and in place. I could clearly recall at that point wondering how to approach the conversation when the previous one in these lines was a downright mockery of God.

I was told in as many words that he still wanted to see the God that would give me a home!

That evening behind the closed bedroom door, I closed my eyes and retreated into the secret place. God's voice roared:

"Do you not know that the earth is mine and the fullness thereof?"

I was about to interrupt and say, "Yes, Father," when He continued:

"Don't interrupt, child! I own the cattle on a thousand hills, and I will not be mocked!"

I fell silent, and so did He.

Now I stand in a place of victory! My God, my Abba Father made a way! He parted that proverbial Red Sea, and the dry land is showing.

Yes, I'm going to just say it – it was a glorious moment!

His initial shock and the disbelief of his facial expression soon subsided to make way for the sneering and gratefulness of my departure. I left it at that.

Many questions were fired in the ensuing days trying to establish where I was going, and did I get the job, and was it more money? Like thousands more? When did I sign the contract?

When is the final date of my departure? And can I please help to make a list of what he needs when I leave?

Silent disbelief enfolded me. I retreated into my world of organizing and coping within.

During the last month or so of my stay in the "madhouse" my domestic lady also fell seriously ill with cancer. I was left to do most of the packing and sorting myself with no assistance. But this also, was just the last of what was left in the house as my life had been packed up systematically over the last two years since I had made my decision and most of my existence stacked in boxes and marked and labelled in an outside part of the house.

Chapter 23
The Exit

18 "Do not remember the past events, pay no attention to things of old.
19 Look, I am about to do something new: even now it is coming. Do you not see it? Indeed, I will make a way in the wilderness, rivers in the desert." – Isaiah 43:18–19

Look forward, onward and upward!

The days leading up to the exit were filled with attempts of trying to convince me to stay. We could have looked and seen if there was a way.

Really, Jezebel? I am done going round this mountain! The time has come for me to train with the racehorses, and I don't run with dead donkeys!

Please understand me clearly – this was one of the hardest and toughest decisions that I had to make in my entire existence. Not even my divorce was such an absolute warrior battle for the prevailing of my pure life in any manner or form.

If it was not for the Abba Father in His glory and goodness in my life, I would never have made it! I share an extract of our conversation the week before my departure.

Liesel, my hand is on next week.
It is our week,
A week of coming together.
A culmination of dreams, tears and

My power coming forth.
It will be the week where my glory.
Will be seen in the manifestation of your life and dreams.
Tangibly, without a doubt.
You too will know that this is my hand that brought it together.

Your freedom was My choice.
Our home was also My choice.
You listened.

(Thank you, Father, You get all the honor!)

The morning of 24 June 2022 arrived. I went through the motions of going to work as for a normal working day. Having packed all my personal belongings I started to do the rounds at 14:00 that day to say my last goodbyes. It was tearful and sad, an era and a door that closed. I knew that this too was a lesson in growth and the opening of my eyes.

I got into my car and drove to the "madhouse" – the last trip I would ever do from the then work to the then so-called home. Two friends and my future daughter-in-law helped me to move all my clothes and personal belongings into their vehicles to take to my new home before the relocation van would arrive the next morning. It was a solemn exercise with only the necessary communication in the house. Tensions could be cut with a knife.

The last night in the "madhouse."

Alone. Silence. Internal questions.

"Stand, child, Stand!"

The relocation van stopped at eight on 25 June 2022. So did my daughter-in-law. When Ronny stepped out of the truck to meet me, he said:

"I remember this. I moved you in here four and a half years ago. That man still said that I would be moving you out here again!"

"You remember that, Ronny?" The proverbial wind taken out of me.

"Yes, I do. Clearly."

"Just goes to show how *words* come full circle, doesn't it!" I left it at that.

The truck was loaded, ready for departure at nine. Both our cars were filled. I did one last round through the empty home, took my set of keys, and placed them on the kitchen counter.

I looked up and saw him coming forward to hug me. I stood.

Turned around – walked through that door I so prayed about and met my daughter-in-law outside. She took my hand, tears running down my face, and together we walked out the gates.

For good. Three years and six days after my first prayer on 19 June 2019.

1 Peter 5:10

"The God of all grace, who called you to his eternal glory in Christ, will himself restore, establish, strengthen, and support you after you have suffered a little while."

Chapter 24
Steadfast

51 "Now it came to pass, when the time had come for Him to be received up, that He steadfastly set His face to go to Jerusalem, 52 and sent messengers before His face. And as they went, they entered a village of the Samaritans, to prepare for Him. 53 But they did not receive Him, because His face was set for the journey to Jerusalem." – Luke 9:51–53 (NKJV)

Setting your face and your walk on that which is ahead.

The first thirty days after deliverance from the "madhouse" I found myself in a period of intense mixed emotions. The enemy's attacks were vile and at the most arbitrary times. I intentionally blocked him from my phone and focused on my re-establishment and finding my way in my new home and in my new position.

The pure joy of having to listen to my messages as loud as I want, having the freedom of movement with all my things around me and filling the kettle as full as I wanted it, (without being told to not fill it to the brim) was absolute heaven on earth!

In this time, I received a message, notifying me that my domestic lady had passed on to be with the Lord. If ever I had confirmation that this season was over, it was that day.

I battled to gain my equilibrium and fought bouts of suppressed anger which would bubble up at the most unexpected moments. From moving in a space of daily fighting for my existence and my right of place as a woman, clawing forward at times in gaining a financial foothold and new life of establishment; I was now standing in it, but my insides were a pulp.

Survival instinct drove the adrenaline, but the emotions were fruit salad in a smoothie maker!

It was time to get to me.

Everyone would tell you, it's hard to start the diet, harder to lose the weight, but hell to maintain and keep the weight off.

This was no different!

I had to crucify the flesh daily, bind and loose and consistently keep reminding myself on **Matthew 6:14:** *"For if you forgive others their offenses, your heavenly Father will forgive you as well."*

Upon having a conversation with the HR assistant at the office, about my anger situation and my unnatural outburst of tears we discussed the possibility of "Stockholm syndrome." At this point I had to admit I hardly had any idea what that was.

Google told me it was a coping mechanism to a captive or abusive situation! People develop positive feelings towards their captors or abusers over time. This condition applies to situations including child abuse, coach-athlete abuse, relationship abuse and sex trafficking.

Oh charming! I, for the first time admitted I needed help, and I needed it fast. For not only was the "madhouse" situation part of the cause, but I pretty much had a double whammy on the career side at the office of my previous employer as well.

Off I went to see the psychologist.

I wasn't crazy. And I wasn't mad as I so often was told.

Through tears and a messy first session it all came out in between heaps of tissues, anger, and uncontrollable sobs!

I had PTSD – post traumatic stress disorder. Period.

No meds, just needed some good self-care, a few sessions of talking it through and a healthy dose of the Word:

Hebrews 10:35–36

35 "So don't throw away your confidence, which has a great reward.

36 For you need endurance, so that after you have done God's will, you may receive what was promised."

Three sessions later and talking through it, I had a clear idea of where I was going next, and the journey was exciting. Doors opened and people entered my life on a whole new trajectory; on a personal level that I never could have envisioned. It was as if suddenly I was in the fast lane and things were moving and moving quickly.

It took great discipline to stay in my lane. To not get sidetracked into the plans of the enemy, living a life of busy-ness, and not making the time for my Abba Father.

Liesel started emerging – and I loved the plan and road ahead of me.

My child,

This is a new season for you.

You've come through the woods and wilderness.

I'm working your healing and I'm pleased to see that you are working with me.

Chapter 25
The Anointing

18 "The Spirit of the Lord is on me, because he has anointed me to preach good news to the poor. He has sent me to proclaim release to the captives and recovery of sight to the blind, to set free the oppressed, 19 to proclaim the year of the Lord's favor." – Luke 4: 18–19
(In red in your Bible, Jesus is speaking)

Anointing makes the difference!

Jesus says that the Spirit of the Lord is upon me because He has anointed me.

When you get into a church or hear someone sing that's really anointed, that is different! It's tangible. It touches a part of you that talent doesn't.

One of the problems with us is, that we can't tell the difference between anointing and great! There's a huge difference. The Bible tells us that it's the anointing that breaks the yoke. It's not planning or natural things that break the yoke of the enemy. It is the anointing.

Jesus said the Spirit of the Lord has come upon me. Anointing is a mantle. It's not something you grow into. It's something that comes on you.

There is a purpose for anointing. Jesus was anointed so people could be healed, delivered, and set free. It wasn't just so people could feel good, be entertained, or have the joy of the presence of the Lord. He said there is a purpose to anointing.

Our problem is we use anointing for entertainment instead of its purpose.

Jesus said, in the verse above:

1. He was anointed to preach the gospel to the poor

When we see the poor, we tend to think they need money. Most of the time it doesn't change their lives.

Remember the saying – "Give a man a fish and he will eat for a day but teach him how to fish and he eats for a lifetime." Jesus knew that. He was anointed not to give the poor money, but to preach the gospel to them. The Word is alive and living and could produce what they needed to change their lives out of poverty into prosperity. There was something in the Word that could break the cycles off their life that kept them there.

This is not just poor in the natural, it is also poor in the Spirit. The Lords says that the gospel breaks that cycle – it changes them.

2. He was anointed to heal the brokenhearted

The word brokenhearted means to be wounded, crushed completely or to shatter. One of the meanings of brokenhearted is that it makes you lose hope! And the Lord says that He is anointed to heal them.

There are things that happen to believers, that break our hearts. And when your heart is broken you cannot fulfill your purpose. The Bible says that out of the heart flows the issues of life. It's your heart that God looks at and when your heart gets broken you can't do what God called you to do. God says that He wants to heal it. He has been anointed to heal the wound.

Whatever has happened to you in your past, some of the greatest wounds come from people that we loved and whom we trusted. When these things happen, it makes you lose your zest of life. It takes your hope away. The Bible says hope is the anchor of your soul. Your soul is your will, mind, and emotions. When you lose your hope, your emotions are no longer anchored, they just drift, and it plays havoc with your life.

Jesus said, the poor need the gospel preached to them, but the brokenhearted need to be healed.

And I'd like to add in right here – that you cannot heal in the place where you were broken!

We have all had wounds where we just want to give up on life. My story isn't any different to yours. God doesn't want that. He said to heal your heart that has been broken.

3. *He was anointed to preach deliverance to the captives*

Captives mean prisoners of war. A prisoner of war is not there by choice. Many of us landed in situations, not by choice; but captured by the enemy.

Jesus says that He has been sent to preach deliverance to the captives. Deliverance means release from prison.

Can you see this? It's different from the good news to the poor.

There is so much bondage today because there is very little preaching on deliverance from captivity any more. I'm talking about preaching with anointing!

There is teaching of the Word for the believer. This is somebody that has accepted Christ and has been saved. Teaching the Word is teaching the principles of God to a believer so that they can mature from milk to meat, so that they can become strong in the Lord.

But people that are prisoners of war, are people that are captive. This can be captivity in drugs, pornography and even gluttony. They have been taken captive. They don't realize that they are in enemy territory.

Teaching is about the believer, but preaching is about the sinner. It's about deliverance if we need to see people set free.

The enemy's greatest work is deception!

4. <u>He was anointed to recover the sight to the blind</u>

The recovery of sight to the blind – not healing. This means that they had sight before, they had sight at one time. The spirit of deception is blindness.

The god of this world has blinded the eyes of the people. Even in the realm of politics. The enemy can blind someone that they can no longer see. We see this in the spirit of Behemoth.

5. <u>He was anointed to set free the oppressed</u>

This is almost synonymous with the brokenhearted. Oppressed meaning to aggrieve, persecute and wrong; to bruise. The opposite of uphold and encourage.

Not all have a heart that is broken. A bruise is an invisible wound. A wound that is on the inside. You are not bleeding but when you look down, there has been a breaking of the blood vessels and it pools under the skin and when you look at that and you see the discoloration – that is a bruise.

The enemy has created some bruises that don't bleed in all of us. The Lord says it will take your liberty away, your freedom from moving into your purpose.

The Bible says that when He was crucified, he was bruised for our transgressions, so that we don't have to endure that any more.

A bruise is very sensitive and tender. You can touch it and it hurts. And yet there's no breaking of the skin. The enemy has bruised us, an invisible wound that people don't see. Yet, when something happens and it touches you, it hurts. God says that He has been anointed to set us free from that bruise.

Jesus is physically gone from the earth. He gave the anointing that He had on Him to you and me. This is our mandate; this is our purpose.

God always anoints for a purpose – it's not for show.

Chapter 26
The Process

22 "The LORD spoke to Moses:
23 Take for yourself the finest spices: 12,5 pounds of liquid myrrh, half as much (6,25 pounds) of fragrant cinnamon, 6,25 pounds of fragrant cane,
24 – 12,5 pounds of cassia (by the sanctuary shekel), and a gallon of olive oil.
25 Prepare from these a holy anointing oil, a scented blend, the work of a perfumer; it will be holy anointing oil." – Exodus 30:22–25

Anointing has Protocol!

According to scripture above there are five ingredients that God required for anointing oil. I'm going to break these down and endeavor to explain the importance and impact. This will clearly now, in hindsight on the previous chapters show why certain steps had to take place.

1. <u>Myrrh</u>

Myrrh was one of the three gifts that was given to Jesus at birth by the three wise men. It was an anointing oil, frankincense as a perfume and gold as a valuable. The three gifts had a spiritual meaning: gold as a symbol of kingship on earth; frankincense (an incense) as a symbol of deity; and myrrh (an embalming oil) as a symbol of death.

Death? Yes, death to self and submission to God. Myrrh gum was extracted from trees when a wound on the tree penetrates through the bark and into the sapwood. The tree secretes the resin. *Myrrh is harvested by repeatedly wounding the trees to bleed the gum.* Through a process the oil was formed, resulting in a sweet-smelling fragrance.

Are you getting this?

Myrrh represents our meekness and submission to God's will, to strengthen and harness us for His service. It's submitting all that you have in obedience to God. This attracts the anointing.

The Bible says that Moses was the meekest man that ever lived. It took one third of his life to get to that place – forty years spent in the wilderness. It was in this period that God taught him faith! It's obedience.

2. *Cinnamon*

Cinnamon is a spice obtained from the inner bark of several tree species from the genus Cinnamomum. These trees grow straight up and have no curves. The fruit is also used to make candles.

Cinnamon is representative of uprightness – how we stand in God. Standing for what is right. Standing for truth.

Added light brings added blessing. Added blessings bring added responsibility. Stand in His righteousness not your own. The basis of your stand is Jesus.

Stand on His promises.

If you don't stand for something, you will fall for anything. It's time to stand. You must stand against the devil, the world, and the flesh.

Get Divine backbone! In Hebrews 11, Moses said, "No" to Egypt and "Yes" to God. You need to start saying no to evil. If you say no to what God says no to, the anointing will flow in your direction. There are some fundamentals that cannot be changed.

Four times in Ephesians God tells us to Stand! When it looks like nothing is working – you don't quit, you don't get angry – you Stand! The Word tells us that if you have done everything you could to stand, stand, therefore. With an upright stand!

3. *Fragrant Cane*

Sweet-smelling Cane is a fragrant reed that grows in swamps with a head filled with oil. It wasn't ready to use until the head was bent over and almost touched the ground. It speaks of bending low in humility.

We must have humility.

Jesus had a level of humility that we don't understand. He bent over to wash the feet of the disciples – the same hands that created the universe! From magnificence to the menial task of foot washing.

If you want to be great – bring your basin, water and towel and wash some feet. Be of service. You must be prepared to bend low in humility and serve people. God says it's not about your popularity, your title, or your name, it's about serving people. The more humility, the more the anointing is drawn.

4. *Cassia*

There are over four hundred types that grow in tropical areas. The main property of this oil is for inner cleansing, an antifungal or antibacterial that gets rid of infections.

If you want anointing, you need inner cleansing. Every now and then you need to bring everything in you to the foot of the cross. Go back to God to search your heart and cleanse you from that which blocks the anointing.

You must clean up your temple. What are you feeding on? What are you reading, listening to, watching, or saying? What are you putting in your mind?

Clean out the noise.

Clean out the workshop of your talents.

Clean up the playroom of your pleasures, pass times and entertainment.

Malachi says that, "He will be like a refiner's fire and purifier of silver."

Philipians 1:6

"I am sure of this, that he who started a good work in you will carry it on to completion until the day of Christ Jesus."

Inner cleansing attracts anointing. God recently told me in one of our morning sessions:

I am removing old bark from your woods,
So, they don't catch fire in your future!

My child,
Eagles don't need to get near trees that are burning.
Take care of all the dead wood,
Throw out, so when the flint strikes again,
The sap of the healthy tree will deflect any fire!

What a word!

5. <u>Olive Oil</u>

Olive Oil represents and speaks of the Holy Spirit.

We must be filled with the Holy Spirit.

Olive Oil was and is still used to cook food – Holy Spirit

feeds us.

Olive Oil was used to bring rest and comfort and was put on feet after a long journey. Holy Spirit is called The Comforter and He anoints our heads with oil, according to Psalm 23.

The Good Samaritan poured olive oil into the wounds of the man that was robbed. It heals wounds and hurts. Holy spirit heals our minds, broken hearts, and relationships.

It was used to anoint kings and prophets. In Psalm 92:10 it speaks of anointing us with fresh oil. Old oil attracts flies and has a stench; it also attracts the enemy. Satan is called the lord of flies. (Matthew 12:24. Beelzebul meaning lord of the flies).

Fighting today's battles with yesterday's oil is a futile thing. Yesterday's oil is miserable as a substitute for fresh oil today.

We need to stay in prayer and continually ask for fresh oil and understanding for a fresh anointing.

Standing in these protocols are crucial to live a life of overcoming. For our strength alone is not sufficient to bring the change we so desire. It is only by the strength and anointing of God that the yoke can be destroyed and we as followers of Jesus Christ can break out of bondage.

Make the choice. You need anointing.

The word says in **Psalm 105:15**

"Do not touch my anointed ones or harm my prophets."

God will deal with the enemy who deals with you, that is what the anointing promises.

Chapter 27
Repeat the Recipe

20 "He who heeds the word wisely will find good, and whoever trusts in the LORD, happy is he." – Proverbs 16:20 (NKJV)

The formula stays the same for every situation!

We now got to grips with some mechanics in the faith to establish a deeper walk with God. To now walk out His purpose for you, towards your destiny.

Part of my healing process was getting back to who I really was, the parts of me that I neglected, my identity that was stolen, my confidence which took a serious beating. I needed to get that part of my being back. To rebuild, to find out what I as a person enjoyed and was good at.

As mentioned in the previous chapters, doors opened that I could never have imagined before. I picked up bonds with friends of many years back, whom, had a journey of their own and was now placed on my road, unaware that they were taking me forward.

In my childhood and a little bit during my years of study, I did very low-key modelling. After my divorce, I found that I had photographic abilities that I never recognized before and started building a portfolio of sorts. During the years in the "madhouse" this was very much recognized and commented on, many a time with derogatory remarks.

Now the opportunities opened again, and I was asked to join a photoshoot for a modelling company. This was the catalyst for what was to follow. A modelling competition presented itself. That same knowingness that sat in my spirit the day I was confronted with the PA competition took hold of me. To this day this is not something I can explain to you. It is an inbuilt urgency of making use of and acknowledging what is in front of me. The age limit for this competition was fifty-five.

I was the first entry in the category.

I had twelve weeks to prepare. All I knew was that I had to do it, for me. Whatever happens after that happens. But I knew I needed help!

Proverbs 19:20

20 "Listen to counsel and receive instruction so that you may be wise later in life."

I went back to the same formula God gave me for the PA competition.

I wrote the plan and made it plain – the Prayer of Petition.

I calculated the cost and prayed for seed;

Sowed into the prayer according to scripture that I stood on; and planned my work and worked my plan

I set out and sought help from various sources:
- A personal trainer.
- Personal modelling classes to update my skill.
- Worked my eating plan and cleaned up my act.
- Researched the requirements for clothes and the theme.
- Found myself a dressmaker and a designer.
- Sourced a hatmaker, feathers and whatever was needed.

My diary was filled with praying, training, preparing meals, work, classes, tanning, praying sleeping and doing it all over again the next day.

Practice, practice, and more practice.

Prayer, decree and fast.

Focused, determined, and driven.

Psalm 37:5–6

5 "Commit your way to the LORD, trust in him, and he will act,

6 making your righteousness shine like the dawn, your justice like the noonday."

Twelve weeks is a long time, but not nearly as long as the previous years.

The day arrived and I travelled to Mossel Bay. My mom flew into Cape Town the day before and a good friend drove with us, in support of this venture. Nervous? Yes, I had a good measure, but I also knew that I gave it my all, in preparation.

It was an early start the next morning, with registration at ten and the competition kicked off at twelve. The first ramp went well, and I was suitably comfortable in my preparation for it. But there was competition. The day was long and grueling. The second and last ramp was at about 19.15 that evening. By now, all fun had escaped me! This ramp was not the one I had the most confidence in, it showed, and I was severely tested.

When it was time for the announcements, I stood at the back and just surrendered the whole thing to God.

They announced me the winner!

I was officially crowned Mrs. Eden SA 2022 Top Model Winner! To God all the glory and all the honor.

I share this story with you so you can get a clear understanding of your part in the faith process. It is not only God that watches from above, who in His might and wisdom is fully able and willing to bless you, but you need to show faith, work, and commitment. There is protocol – there is God's way.

And trust me – The mechanics of God work.

Chapter 28
Eagles

"For the prudent the path of life leads upward, so that he may avoid going down to Sheol." – Proverbs 15:24

Stagnation is not the Will of God, Growth is our inheritance!

Sheol in the Old Testament is the word that is used for the place of the dead. It is derived from a word meaning hollow in Hebrew.

Psalm 88:3–4 says:

3 "For I have had enough troubles, and my life is near Sheol.
4 I am counted among those going down to the Pit."

God continually in scriptures calls us to come up higher. Jesus himself was said to have grown in stature and in favor with God. (Luke 2:52)

It is our calling to continually grow! If you are in the same place naturally and spiritually as last year, and the year before that and the year before that, something is desperately wrong! It is time to take stock of your life.

On 20 October 2022, in our morning discussion time God spoke these words to me:

Your standards are rising – it is time.
But Liesel, they need to rise more – a lot more.
You need to fly, and you haven't taken off yet.
Remember child the runway for the jet is to get momentum

to lift and then stay in the air.
You are gaining momentum.
Stay fed on My Word.
Create that healthy balance child.
Set your boundaries and push when you need to push.

We reach a point in our lives where we must consciously decide to be done with the chickens in the hen house! Just done! No arguing, no deliberation, just done.

Turning our focus upward and onward and to do whatever it takes to acquire the character and habits of an eagle. The Bible often uses the symbol of an eagle to portray strength, power, vision and even destruction. The Biblical analogies using eagles should inspire us to righteous living and strengthen our walk with God!

Isaiah 40:31

"But those who trust in the Lord will renew their strength; they will soar on wings like eagles; they will run and not become weary, they will walk and not faint."

On further research about eagles, I found these characteristics of an eagle fascinating:

1. Eagles fly alone at high altitude.

(Associate with people who are at your level, or those who can help you to grow.)

2. Eagles fly with their own kind.

(Find people who think like you, so that you can both dream and grow together.)

3. Eagles have vision, amazing eyesight, and concentration.

(Do the same with your goals. Focus on accomplishing one thing at a time.)

4. Eagles are fearless and never surrender to the size or strength of their prey.

(Don't give in to the wiles of the enemy.)

5. Eagles are tenacious.

(Be fierce in your pursuit of God's promises in your life.)

6. Eagles never eat dead things. They feed on live meat.

(Don't waste your energy beating a dead horse!)

7. Eagles love the storm; they know the storm winds will lift them above the clouds.

Here they can rest their wings and become stronger.

(Know that adversity is the ideal opportunity to rise.)

8. Eagles test the level of commitment before engagement. The female eagle tests her male suitors to establish his level of commitment.

(It is wise to ascertain the commitment of people we intend to partner with.)

9. Eagles prepare for training and are masters of change management. The mother eagle carefully prepares the nest for its eggs. When it is time for the eaglet to learn to fly, the mother begins to remove the comfort layers from the nest, exposing the pricks and sticks. She then throws the eaglets out of the nest. She does this repeatedly until the eaglet learns to fly.

(We must not become complacent in life, clinging to the old and familiar. We can only grow if we are willing to step out of our comfort zone.)

10. Eagles possess vitality.

(Scripture says in God we find strength. Stay in the Word)

11. Eagles are at the top of the food chain.

(There is no higher way than that of the Abba Father. His ways are higher than ours and His thoughts are higher than ours)

12. The eagle must make a painful decision at around forty.

Die or go through a painful process of rebirth which will extend its life for thirty more years. This process involves the painful task of knocking out its own beak and plucking out its talons so that new ones can grow. This entire process takes approximately five months to complete.

(Many of us want success or change, but without the sacrifice, hard work, disappointments, and heartbreak that comes with it. To survive and grow, we must be willing to change. And sometimes, we may even need to go a step further – a death of the old self and a total rebirth. Ending toxic relationships, leaving toxic jobs, getting rid of destructive habits, thoughts, traditions, and mind-sets that no longer serve us.)

Eagles represent honesty, truth, majesty, strength, courage, wisdom, power, and freedom.

In its youth, the eagle has instinct, but no skill. He has desire but he is not yet ready to go it totally alone. If the eaglet thinks he is ready, and leaves the care of its parents, it most likely will not survive. So just as an eaglet must wait on its parents, we must learn to wait patiently upon the Lord!

Is it any wonder that Abba Father continuously nudges and urges us to come up higher, where the view is better, the air is clearer and the way is above the storm, where our wings can rest and grow stronger.

Deuteronomy 32:11

"He watches over his nest like an eagle and hovers over his young; he spreads his wings, catches him and carries him on his feathers."

Chapter 29
Stay In Your Lane

1 "LORD, you have searched me and known me
2 You know when I sit down and when I stand up; you understand my thoughts from far away.
3 You observe my travels and my rest; you are aware of all my ways.
4 before a word is on my tongue, you know all about it, LORD.
5 You have encircled me; you have placed you hand on me.
6 This wondrous knowledge is beyond me. It is lofty; I am unable to reach it.
7 Where can I go to escape your Spirit? Where can I flee from your presence?
8 If I go up to heaven. You are there; if I make my bed in Sheol, you are there.
9 If I live at the eastern horizon or settle at the western limits,
10 even there your hand will lead me; your right hand will hold on to me.
Psalm 139: 1–10

You don't need to see the full staircase, just take the next step.

1. <u>He is the light and shines the light upon your ways</u>

When we drive in a vehicle at night, we only see the few hundred meters in front of us in the headlights at night. We don't see the end of the road for that journey, but we do see enough to continually move forward as far as the headlights allow us to see in the immediate distance. As we continue forward the headlights light up the next few hundred meters and so forth until we reach the end of the journey.

The same principle applies in our walk with Jesus in this journey of life. At any given time, He allows us to plan our journey, but we walk in the unfolding of the journey a few steps at a time. He allows us to see only a few meters ahead of us, to stay encouraged and uplifted. It is therefore cardinally important to stay grafted in the vine and heed to the living Word daily.

Psalm 119:105 says:

"Your word is a lamp for my feet and a light on my path."

2. *He satisfies your hunger*

Ask God for more of a desire for Him in your daily life.

Psalm 34:10

"Young lions lack food and go hungry, but those who seek the Lord will not lack good thing."

This will lead into a life of intimacy with Him, relationship and living in Him with a deepening of your walk. We can't get more of God. He is in us, but we can get deeper in a relationship with Him.

Christian is not God's word for us – that is a secular word. God's word for us is "in Christ." Not Christlike. If you are in Christ, you spend time with Christ, so you can be like Christ. This is not a play of words; it's a game changer to what God is trying to reveal to us!

John 3:16 says:

"For God loved the world in this way; He gave his one and only Son, so that everyone who believes in him will not perish but have eternal life."

It is for whoever *believes in Him* – not behaves!

The Bible mentions the word Christian three times, but "in Christ" more than seventy times. To classify and call yourself a good person does not make you a Christian or a believer.

Paul wrote most of the New Testament and his writings always refer to "in Jesus." He made a big deal about Jesus. Where did he get the revelation from?

When he persecuted Christians," the Bible says that Jesus asked him: "Why are you persecuting me?" Jesus didn't relate to Christians; He is *in* Christians. The Bible says, God *in* you the hope of glory! This opened Paul's eyes; it opened a world.

Jesus is not somebody that I try to connect to. It's somebody that I live in. It's us being in Jesus and He in us.

You can change everything in your life by applying Christian principles in your life. But the core of who you are is never changed, *until* we get Jesus. Our purpose is to seek Him.

3. *He speaks, be quiet*

Ask to hear his voice. He will speak. The word tells us this.

1 Kings 19:12

"After the earthquake there was a fire, but the Lord was not in the fire. And after the fire there was voice, a soft whisper."

Abba Father does not contend with noise. He does not lift His voice to shout and scream above the busy-ness of your day.

He loved you enough and gave you the ability of free choice.

A choice to make room for Him.

A choice to choose the silence over the noise.

A choice to allow Him the freedom to speak into your life – in an audible voice that you will hear and understand when you seek deeper intimacy with Him.

John 10:27

"My sheep hear my voice, I know them, and they follow me."

4. Rejoice

Romans 12:12

"Rejoice in hope; be patient in affliction, be persistent in prayer."

Live a life of expectancy!

Expect the breakthrough.

Expect the miracle.

Expect that it be on earth as it is in heaven in your life.

In this lies hope and joy – it cultivates the atmosphere for a miracle to manifest.

James 1: 2–4:

2 *"Consider it a great joy, my brothers, and sisters, whenever you experience various trials,*

3 *because you know that the testing of your faith produces endurance.*

4 *And let endurance have its full effect, so that you may be mature and complete, lacking nothing."*

Chapter 30
Paying It Forward

"The LORD God took the man and placed him in the garden of Eden to work it and watch over it." – Genesis 2:15

Walking in your revealed purpose and life.

God, the Father, did not create birds until he created air, neither did he create fish until he created water. Man was created after the earth and the environment he had to live in, was established. God always creates the element of environment before the living creature.

God made the crib before the baby was laid into it. The crib for humanity was the Garden of Eden. It was more than just a place to live or a sanctuary to dwell in – it was the place of unity, the coming together of the spiritual world and the natural (earthly) world. A place of God's earthly family. This was the place where these two worlds overlapped. Adam's world was in the garden, the haven of safety and provision, until through sin he was exiled from that place.

All children were and are born out of the garden. Every descendant of Adam came outside of God's presence and outside of the relationship with God. Therefore "bad" comes naturally to the human nature. We descend from Adam. But God…! God worked a plan to reconcile us and bring us back into Jesus.

The Bible tells us that God is the vinedresser (John 15:1) and that He sent the vine (Jesus) to be planted in the earth. God then takes Christians and plants them into Jesus Christ. But we cannot get into Jesus until we step out and away from Adam.

How?

Jesus died and took care of our sins on the cross. This was a divine exchange of His spotless blood that was shed for our sins, to reconcile us back into Him. That means that we die to self, our old nature gets buried, we get born again by the baptism and we are resurrected *into* new life with Jesus as our King.

Through Jesus there is access to new life. Our goal is to get people from Adam to the cross.

There is life in Him. He who has the Son has life, according to scripture.

A lightbulb has everything it needs to create life and to shine. But unless that lightbulb is connected and placed into the socket there is no light! The same applies in Jesus.

Abide in Him! Don't profess it, possess it. He is not our supplement or vitamins. He is The Source. He is vital to our existence.

Philippians 4:13

'I am able to do all things through him who strengthens me."

The only distance between you and the Father is your unawareness of his nearness. Everyone who abides in Him, will pray. But not everyone who prays, abides in Him. You can only abide through birth, either in Adam or in Christ.

For God, my Abba Father loves you so much –

He gave you choice!

Chapter 31
Conclusion

"Let us run with endurance the race that lies before us. 2 keeping our eyes on Jesus, the source and perfecter of our faith. For the joy that lay before him, he endured the cross, despising the shame, and sat down at the right hand of the throne of God." – Hebrews 12:1–2

This book was not of my own doing.

It was a clear instruction and assignment from the Father. I share the instruction on 6 December 2022:

We will write, child,
But it will come in rest.
It will flow with my spirit and my atmosphere.

Cleanse your house, child.

For this is great work.
A work that will go before you and help others.
A desperately needed work.
My way needs to be spoken and there for all to know and see.
I will no longer tolerate the oppression of my children.
I am raising up a people that will know how to overcome.
They will hear my voice,

Partner with me to conquer evil on this earth.
Not only in your nation.

For the time has come for my Esther's to rise
And fight for My way and My will.

It took me seven days to write from cover to cover, through tears, violent sobbing and seeking scripture. Only knowing the next two to three chapters per day, just like the headlights in the road.

Through this came not only internal healing, closing of doors and revelation upon revelation, but a new understanding of obedience and a deeper walk of faith.

It brought trust, discernment, and a new level of knowing who I am *in* Him, and not only Him in me.

I share this humbly, with great expectation that this will change lives. That being radical for God will become your normal.

I pray over you: –

Hinds' feet that you may be able to *stand* firmly and tread safely on paths of testing and trouble.

The mind of Christ that you may discern in wisdom and make the God way your choice in every situation.

Strengthened wings that you may soar above the clouds.

The breath of God to keep you in the air.

I gift you a white rose of peace as a symbol of God's peace that surpasses all understanding and that it be grafted in you wherever you go.

And I wish for you the wonder of recognition.

That you may be recognized as an eagle, and someone also call you – Aquila.

NOTES

I share here some notes of interest to clarify and provide insight on various aspects of terminology, to create a deeper understanding.

1. All scripture quoted in this book is quoted from The Christian Standard Bible, which does differ in various language differentiations to the KJV and the NKJV. Where applicable I have indicated where the NKJV was referred to.

2. *The use of the words, lord vs Lord vs LORD.*

lord: All lower case is representing the word adon (meaning to rule). This is for referral to men and not God.

Lord: This in normal type is the Hebrew translation for Adonai, meaning, my Lord.

LORD: This is God's Hebrew name YHWH (pronounced Yahweh or Yehova) and refers to self-Existent or Eternal.

3. Christ means "The Anointed One." So, therefore, to be *in* Christ means to be anointed.

4. In Prayers of Petition, I refer to God by various names. When praying for various incidents or requirements, I have come into the habit of praying to that part or name of God's character and name relating to that specific request. I provide herewith a short summary of some the names of Jesus:

- El Shaddai – Lord God Almighty (The God of more than enough)
- El Elyon – The Most High God
- Adonai – Lord, Master

- Yahweh – Lord, Jehovah
- Jehovah Nissi – The Lord my Banner
- Jevovah Raah – The Lord my Shepherd
- Jehovah Rapha – The Lord that Heals
- Jehovah Shammah – The Lord is There
- Jehovah Tsidkenu – The Lord our Righteousness
- Jehovan Mekoddishkem – The Lord who sanctifies you.
- El Olam – The Everlasting God
- Elohim – God
- Jehovah Jireh – The Lord will Provide
- Jehovah Shalom – The Lord is Peace
- Jehovah Sabaoth – The Lord of Hosts